Kayaking the Texas Coast

Number Eighteen: Gulf Coast Books

Sponsored by
Texas A&M University–Corpus Christi

John W. Tunnell Jr., General Editor

*A list of other titles available in this series
appears at the end of the book.*

KAYAKING THE
TEXAS COAST

John Whorff

TEXAS A&M UNIVERSITY PRESS

This paper meets the requirements of
ANSI/NISO, Z39.48-1992
(Permanence of Paper).
Binding materials have been
chosen for durability.

Library of Congress Cataloging-in-Publication Data

Whorff, John, 1964–
   Kayaking the Texas coast / John Whorff. — 1st ed.
      p. cm. — (Gulf Coast books ; no. 18)
   Includes index.
   ISBN-13: 978-1-60344-225-1 (flexbound : alk. paper)
   ISBN-10: 1-60344-225-1 (flexbound : alk. paper)
1. Sea kayaking—Texas—Gulf Coast—Guidebooks.
2. Gulf Coast (Tex.)—Guidebooks.
I. Title.   II. Series: Gulf Coast books ; no. 18.

GV776.T42G98   2011
797.122'4—dc22

2010020846

DISCLAIMER

Although every effort has been made to assure the accuracy and reliability of the information presented in this book, readers should note that kayaking is a sport with inher-
ent dangers and uncertainties caused by wind, tides, currents, other vessels, and other
aspects of the natural environment. The author and Texas A&M University Press assume
no liability for any injury, disability, or death attendant to or connected with the activities
described in this book.

Contents

Acknowledgments

This book is the product of many years of work. It would not have been possible without the love and encouragement of my wife, Lori, and our two sons, Connor and Jarret. It likewise would not have been finished without the friendship and spiritual guidance of Pastor Henry Suche at our Tuesday morning coffee klatch. Early inspiration came from Ron Duke of Mountain Sports in Kerrville following a feature article I wrote on one of our trips in the December 1999 issue of *Sea Kayaker* magazine. Special thanks to Tom Bochow for keeping me alive during a December 2001 trip to Cedar Bayou when an unexpected storm arose. Tom, Bob Wilson, and Dar Vodjani helped with numerous trips and gave great advice. Without their inspiration and camaraderie this book would not have been possible. Thanks go to everyone who contributed information on routes that we were able to put in this book.

Of all the people who helped me, Ken Johnson was the most significant. He has helped work out routes, contributed GPS information, and provided a variety of pictures. Ken is a legendary figure in the sport. He even has a Mayan Seas boat in production that bears his name. At the time of writing he is seventy-seven years of age and still paddles more than sixty miles each week to stay in shape. For five years we have shared adventures all over the coast with many interesting people. We have paddled together in heavy surf, in adverse weather conditions, and even at night on some of the routes in this book. He is a great friend and a hero on the water (see *Sea Kayaker* magazine, issue 117, April 2007). Thank you Ken!

Kayaking the Texas Coast

Boy Scout Troop 180, from the East Texas Area Council, paddling around the USS Lexington *and along North Beach at Corpus Christi.*

PART 1

SEA KAYAKING IN TEXAS

Sea Kayaking in Texas

THE SPORT OF SEA KAYAKING IS IN ITS infancy in Texas. From Alaska to California on the west coast, from Maine to Florida on the east coast, and even around the Great Lakes, the sport has been popular for years and numerous guidebooks have been published. When paddling along the Texas coast in 1988, I never saw another sea kayak. Now the sport is growing rapidly on the Gulf Coast and is being promoted aggressively by government agencies and conservation groups. Why the promotion? Besides sea kayaks, no other water craft can provide such low impact access to shallow bayshore habitats. Scientists have recognized that the propellers of shallow draft recreational boats and the dragging of shrimp trawls are in part responsible for destruction of sea grass and other benthic communities. For this reason the Texas Parks and Wildlife Department and other agencies have encouraged the kayaking by sponsoring the development of trails along many Texas bays. Maps have become available with GPS coordinates for navigational markers placed in the bays to aid kayakers. Yet there are no comprehensive Texas guides to familiarize novices with

At Corpus Christi kayakers paddle against a city backdrop.

where they can paddle and camp, what they might see, and where they can obtain additional information to enhance their experience and make it safer. The purpose of this guide is to provide a basic framework for novices interested in pursuing the sport and to provide more experienced kayakers with route descriptions and pertinent information on paddling Texas.

Sandy bars and barrier islands fringe many of the shorelines along the Atlantic and Gulf of Mexico. Half of the nearly 400-mile Texas coastline is flanked by sandy barrier islands. Thousands of miles of shoreline surround the shallow bays, lagoons, and islands of the Texas coast. Many barrier island chains have formed along this coast during the past million years, corresponding to changes in shoreline position associated with rising and falling sea level. Although remnants of old shorelines exist, the current barrier island chain was formed less than 5,000 years ago when sea level rose at the end of the Holocene marine transgression. The sands include subtidal Pleistocene and Holocene deposits as well as sand discharged from rivers. Today's islands are the product of these sands washed along a shallow submarine slope with consistent wave action, low tidal amplitude, and longshore currents.

The seaward edges of the barrier islands are lined with sand dune communities with a grassy interior, while lagoons, marshes, and shell beaches lie behind them. The islands are separated by passes where dolphins and turtles are often seen. To accommodate commercial shipping, some of the passes have been widened and deepened, and the Gulf Intracoastal Waterway has been dredged behind the barrier islands along the entire coast. Many of the natural passes have closed due to the resulting changes in bay circulation. With all of the recreation, commercial fishing, industrial development, and maritime transportation comes trash. On many parts of the coast the locals have organized successful cleanup efforts. Many of the bays are much cleaner than I remember twenty years ago. However, Gulf of Mexico beaches that are inaccessible are loaded with trash. Much of this comes from our neighbors to the south. Much of this also comes from careless fishermen and recreational boaters. I hope those of you who read this book and travel to some of these remote

places will practice leave-no-trace ethics. In fact, I challenge all of you who visit the coast to pick up any trash you might see every time you visit. Greater efforts are warranted.

Since the sandy shores along the Texas coast are in general so shallow and gradually sloping, up to three or four shallow bars separated by deeper troughs often parallel the shoreline. The bars can move inshore or offshore depending on the intensity of wave action. For example, storm waves can pull sand offshore and bars will form farther out. Gaps between the bars are formed by rip tides, where water from onshore surf retreats seaward. Both the troughs and areas of rip tides can be utilized by sea kayakers as wave action diminishes in these areas. I have used the central part of rip tides to launch and move safely offshore. I have also utilized the edges of rip tides to make landings when I wanted to avoid heavy surf. During the winter, inshore troughs can often be used to provide refuge from large breaking waves when paddling along the outer coast. Also where surf has become too large to negotiate, I have paddled along shallow troughs just off the beach parallel to shore to make progress to the next pass.

During the calmer summer months longshore currents move primarily northward along most of the outer coast with winds prevailing out of the south-southeast. The rest of the year, although variable, longshore currents converge between Big Shell and Little Shell beaches on Padre Island National Seashore about 50 miles north of the Rio Grande River. This means that strong longshore currents affecting sediment transport generally move south along most of the Texas coast. At the point of convergence between Big Shell and Little Shell beaches, longshore bars and troughs do not parallel the shoreline but form obliquely to it, creating what fisherman call "blind guts," where the currents collide and move offshore. The area is known for very rough waters and numerous shipwrecks. The beaches are coarse and steep with lots of shell accumulation.

Primary and secondary bays have formed behind the barrier islands, producing extensive estuarine marshes, oyster reef communities, and sea grass meadows. Along the central and north coast, where river discharge is greater, there are patches and ridges of winding, jagged oyster reefs with extensive marshes lining the estuarine bays. The shallow bays and lagoons are teeming with wildlife; a birdwatcher's and angler's paradise. The latter is in large part due to the ambitious efforts of the Texas Coastal Conservation Association (CCA-Texas) and the Texas Parks and Wildlife Department. In addition the Galveston Bay Plan was implemented beginning in 1995. The science-based program is administered by the Texas Commission on Environmental Quality and co-ordinates efforts by government agencies, universities, conservation organizations, businesses, industry, and citizens who are interested in protecting and restoring this bay system.

Red drum and speckled sea trout populations are at record levels compared to eighteen years ago. In addition to the numerous shorebirds, gulls, terns, and pelicans, the extensive salt lagoons and coastal marshes have some of the finest waterfowl assemblages in the country. A large proportion of North American birds that spend their winters in the tropics can be seen seasonally on the Texas coast. Small islands and sections of bayshore are often lined with coarse oyster shell beaches. Red bay and live oak trees living in deep sandy soil are often shaped by prevailing Gulf winds into dense thickets called mottes. These and other thickets lend shelter to deer, javelina, feral pigs, coyotes, bobcats, and raccoons. Marshy shoreline habitats are ideal for birds because they provide rich feeding grounds and are in close proximity to the central North American flyway. Alligators are not uncommon in many of these areas.

Sea grass communities are more prevalent along the central and south coast. Especially in the south, there are cactus-covered islands in the shallow, often hyper-saline bays and lagoons with extensive sea grass meadows. Interesting sand dune communities rise up along some of the bayshores as well as the open coast. Some of these isolated sand dune communities are rarely visited and are host to a variety of interesting wildlife. Fortunately, much of the Texas coast has been protected from development by county and state parks, national wildlife refuges, Padre Island National Seashore, conservation groups such as the Audubon Society and Nature Conservancy, and large private landholders like the King and Kenedy ranches.

Few experiences compare with navigating a sea kayak through a large sandy bay lined with cactus on oyster shell beaches, past golden sand dunes into rough ocean waters, then surfing back onto a wind-swept beach at sunset. There is much to be enjoyed camping out of a kayak in the solitude of isolated shoreline communities abundant with wildlife and seldom seen by others.

The intensity of wave action can move sand bars either inshore or offshore.

Kayaks and Equipment

Choosing the proper boat can be difficult. The wrong choice can ruin the sport for a novice. Generally, **touring boats or "sea kayaks"** are 14 to 21 feet long and less than 24 inches wide. They usually have two bulkheads that separate fore and aft compartments from the cockpit to provide dry storage and buoyancy in the event of capsize. One important criterion for these boats is that the hatches and bulkheads do not leak. Many of the boats come with rudders or retractable skegs. There is considerable discussion among experts about which is better or whether either is even necessary. This and the materials, shape, and efficiency of hulls are discussed at length in the following books:

Derek C. Hutchinson, *The Complete Book of Sea Kayaking,* 5th edition (Falcon Publishing, 2004)

Shelley Johnson, *The Complete Sea Kayaker's Handbook* (Ragged Mountain Press, 2002)

Andy Knapp, *The Optimum Kayak* (International Marine/Ragged Mountain Press, 1999)

David Seidman, *The Essential Sea Kayaker* (Ragged Mountain Press, 2001)

After getting an idea of what kind of boat might be best, you can help to narrow down the options by looking at boat reviews in *Sea Kayaker* magazine. These are excellent and are available online (www.seakayakermag.com) or by buying back issues. Always paddle several boats that interest you before making a final decision. Novices can benefit from taking classes first (see Kayak Resources).

Undecked boats or kayaks with an open cockpit are often referred to as "sit-on-tops." These boats are usually plastic and inexpensive to buy, can easily be rented along the coast, and are popular among fishermen. However, most such kayaks are slow and not suitable for multiday trips or rough water. For example, two fishermen in the Port Aransas area died after capsizing in rough water in 2008. There are exceptions, though.

I grew up paddling a sit-on-top called a Royak, which I used on multiday trips, in the surf, and when SCUBA diving on the West Coast. Three of the four boats my family bought in 1971 are still seaworthy, and now my children are paddling them occasionally. These were the first sit-on-top boats ever designed and are still produced today in Sacramento, California. The prototype for the boat was designed by Roy Grabenauer in 1968. On quiet bayous and protected bays canoes may be used. However, their use should be limited to these areas and short distances. They are generally inappropriate for the windswept bays and rough waters of the open coast.

Paddles for touring kayaks are usually between 210 and 230 cm long. Shorter paddles are generally more efficient for a faster cadence or with boats that do not track well (i.e., that have little keel) and are preferred by those who race. I personally prefer a 240 cm length with a very solid blade. The longer paddle provides more leverage when bracing and rolling in surf conditions, and the heavier blade is useful in the shallows, where I often use the paddle to push myself over shallow bars or oyster reefs.

Learning to use a "feathered" paddle is essential as the Texas coast is often a very windy place. The blades on a feathered paddle are placed at an angle to each other. When the paddle is in use, the blade out of the water is angled so that the narrow edge is leading into the wind. This reduces wind resistance and increases efficiency. This means the paddle has to be twisted slightly for each stroke; an unfeathered paddle may be better for those with wrist problems. Paddles are constructed out of differing materials and there are many blade designs available from a variety of manufacturers.

Most sea kayakers wear a type III **personal floatation device (PFD)**. Some of the new designs fit snugly but allow freedom of arm movement and often have large mesh pockets suitable for carrying flares, a radio, and other small items requiring quick access. They also are designed to fit with a variety of spray skirts. PFDs give paddlers buoyancy, insulation, and some degree of protection.

Spray skirts on touring boats are essential in rough water or surf. They also provide sun protection and insulation. Spray skirts are designed to keep water out of the cockpit when maneuvering through rough water or surf or when capsizing. I personally prefer a neoprene skirt with a nylon tunnel.

Other important equipment improves comfort and safety. Serious kayakers have a bilge pump, either built into the boat or portable. Most carry a portable pump with a flotation collar that mounts to the deck.

Dry bags provide waterproof storage for dry clothes, camping equipment, food, and other supplies. Various kinds of jackets are available that provide insulation and help to keep paddlers dry without restricting arm movement. Wetsuits are often necessary between December and February. Paddling gloves and pogies (gloves that mount to the paddle shaft) are important to keep hands warm during the colder months and to help prevent blisters.

To obtain additional information on boats and equipment, see one or more of the books listed in the first paragraph of this section and/or visit your local kayak shop (see Kayak Resources). For novices lessons are essential before buying a boat.

Coastal fog is disorienting but also magical.

Safety Considerations and Emergencies

Float Plan

Judgment is always as important as paddling skill on the Texas coast. When planning a trip, make sure that the proposed route, conditions, and time available do not exceed the capabilities of the weakest member of your group. It is important to plan the trip carefully by formulating a "float plan." This plan should be given to a responsible family member, friend, or park ranger before embarking. A good example of a float plan form can be downloaded for free from "Resources" at the *Sea Kayaker* magazine website (www.seakayakermag.com). Generally a float plan should include the following:

(1) Search and rescue agency to be called if the group does not report in by a given time and date

(2) Detailed description of the kayakers, including pertinent medical history, emergency contacts, skill level, and kayak colors

(3) List of signaling devices (e.g., strobes, flares, light sticks, mirrors, markers, Emergency Position Indicating Radio Beacon or EPIRB), communications gear (VHF radio with call sign or cell phone number with hours of daily monitoring), and equipment (tent colors, first aid kit, fire starting materials, food and water)

(4) Launch and landing sites with proposed route, campsites, and alternatives

(5) Vehicles (make, model, color) or shuttle service contacts

Emergencies

Cell phones generally work well along much of the Texas coast. In case of an emergency, it is important to have the number of the closest U.S. Coast Guard station and sheriff's department along your intended route programmed into your phone. If you are carrying a VHF radio, use channel 16 for help from the Coast Guard and other boaters in the area. The Coast Guard also uses VHF channel 22 to broadcast severe weather warnings, hazards to navigation, and other safety warnings. There are seven Coast Guard stations along the Texas coast:

Port Isabel 956-761-2669
Corpus Christi 361-939-6200
Port Aransas 361-749-5217
Port O' Connor 512-983-2617
Freeport 409-233-7551
Galveston 409-766-5633
Sabine 409-971-2194

Weather and Tides

Air temperatures from November to March average in the 60s and 70s (degrees Fahrenheit) during the day and 40s and 50s at night, according to 1971–2000 National Weather Service data base records from Brownsville, Corpus Christi, and Galveston. From April

Wind and waves can come up very suddenly on the Texas coast. While this can be fun for the experienced, it can pose a significant threat to those untrained or unprepared. Photo by Ken Johnson

to October, temperatures average in the 80s and 90s during the day and 60s and 70s at night. Water temperatures range from 50 to 85 degrees. Scattered thunderstorms are common all year (see recommended lightning safety guidelines). Winter storms bring strong winds out of the north, but prevailing winds are out of the east or southeast for much of the year along the Texas coast. Winds along the coast typically range from 5 to 25 knots. Water currents generated by wind have more influence on bay circulation patterns than does either tidal fluctuation or river discharge, and they can alter predicted tidal levels by as much as a foot and a half. This may not seem like much, but the maximum depth in Aransas Bay is about 13 feet and depth is considerably less in most other bays. Tides fluctuate by about 3 feet in the major passes and a little less in the bays. Many of the natural passes along the Texas coast have closed as a result of the low tidal amplitude combined with the development of deepwater passes and the Gulf Intracoastal Waterway. Tidal currents in the major passes can occasionally be strong, especially in June and December during maximal tide fluctuations. For trip planning, tide predictions can be obtained online for most areas from the National Oceanic and Atmospheric Administration, or NOAA (http://co-ops.nos.noaa.gov/tide_pred.html). For Port Aransas, see the University of Texas Marine Science Institute website (http://nearshore.utmsi.utexas.edu/). Also, tide predictions and marine weather forecasts can be obtained from Weather Underground (http://www.wunderground.com/MAR/txm.html).

Weather can change rapidly along the Texas coast. For multiday trips it is important to monitor the weather. Reports are updated by the National Weather Service every few hours. For pre-trip planning, consult the marine forecasts by phone or online. On a trip, monitor the weather radio frequencies (discussed later) or call the National Weather Service by cell phone. NOAA Weather Radio broadcasts are made on one of seven high-band FM frequencies ranging from 162.40 to 162.55 megahertz. Weather radios with a range of 40–50 miles work on most of the coast. These radios are inexpensive and readily available at most outdoor supply stores. It may be difficult to pick up a signal in some areas, especially south of Baffin Bay.

National Weather Service Forecasts:

Houston/Galveston, 281-337-5074, www.srh.noaa.gov/hgx/

Corpus Christi, 361-289-1861 or 0753, www.srh.noaa.gov/crp/

Brownsville, 956-546-5378, www.srh.noaa.gov/bro/

Navigation

Barrier islands and bayshores are low-lying terrain. From the perspective of a kayaker, distances are deceiving and landmarks are often indiscernible. Good map and compass skills are essential. The maps included in this text are to help guide paddlers but must not be considered a replacement for nautical maps. GPS markers have been placed by the Texas Parks and Wildlife Department to aid navigation along several bay routes. Along the entire length of the coast, intracoastal waterway markers can be used on maps for reference. When paddling, try to stay to the outside of all channel markers, shipping lanes in the passes, and the intracoastal waterway. The following maps are useful for navigation in conjunction with this book:

(1) Waterproof Maps by Hook-N-Line Map Company, 1014 Hercules Ave., Houston, TX 77058, 281-286-6554 (www.hooknline.com)

(2) Waterproof Photomaps and Photocards by Shoreline Publishing, 9337-B Katy Freeway, #176, Houston, TX 77024, 713-973-1627

◄ GPS receivers can be useful for navigation, especially in the bays. Several areas along the coast have photomaps available with GPS markers.

▼ The GPS markers are useful but should not be relied upon because they often get damaged or removed.

▶ Crossing ship channels is dangerous and should be undertaken only by experienced paddlers and only with great care.

▼ When paddling, try to stay to the outside of channel markers, shipping lanes, and the intracoastal waterway.

▼▼ Barges can be difficult to hear as they approach and can wash boats off beaches along the Gulf Intracoastal Waterway.

(3) *Padre Island National Seashore, Texas #251,* Trails Illustrated, P.O. Box 4357, Evergreen, CO 80437–4357, 800-962-1643, (www.maps.nationalgeographic.com)

(4) NOAA nautical charts, NOAA Office of Coast Survey, 1315 East West Highway, Silver Spring, MD 20852, 888–990-NOAA, (www.nauticalcharts.noaa.gov/)

(5) A. P. Balder, *Mariner's Atlas: Texas Gulf Coast* (Houston: Lone Star Books, 1987), 103 pp., Texas Reference Sources Online (www.txla.org/pubs/trs/TBK.html)

(6) Digital Images available from TerraServer.com (www.terraserver.com; by subscription)

(7) Digital Images from Google Earth (www.earth.google.com) and MapQuest (mapquest.com)

I have found the waterproof Hook-N-Line fishing maps and Shoreline Publishing's waterproof aerial maps of the paddling trails to be the most useful. I have also used aerial maps downloaded free from several sources, printed on waterproof paper or put in a waterproof map case. The route maps presented in this book should never be used alone to navigate coastal waters.

Hazards

Sea kayaking is an inherently dangerous sport with unavoidable risks that all paddlers assume when they embark on the water. Unless you have basic boat-handling and seamanship skills, do not attempt any of these routes. Even routes for novice paddlers can be dangerous, depending on the weather or sea conditions and any boat or ship traffic present. Risks can be minimized by being properly equipped, well trained, and physically conditioned. Understand your status in these areas and know your limitations. If possible, paddle with people who are more experienced.

Boat and Ship Traffic

While intracoastal waterway and shipping lane markers are useful aids to navigation, larger pleasure boats, oil industry crew boats, barges, tankers, and cargo ships pose a significant hazard. On a paddling trip a few years ago, my partner and I thought we would stop at an intracoastal waterway buoy marker to consult our map and confirm our position. No boat traffic was noticeable in either direction. We rafted up facing in the direction we intended to paddle on what we thought was the outside of the waterway. We heard the faint sound of an air horn behind us, and we turned just in time to see the monolithic bow of a steel barge bearing down on us less than 100 feet away. The enormous steel hulls of the barges muffled the sound of the workboat pushing them more than two football fields behind the bow. To larger boats and ships, kayakers are invisible! Even when pilots do see a kayaker, they often cannot slow down or maneuver quickly to avoid a collision. I was once told by a friend running a charter boat out of Port Aransas that I looked like a flock of birds on his radar when I crossed his path one night. Stay well clear of larger boat and ship traffic and be as visible as you can.

Lightning

Lightning is a significant hazard on the Texas coast because scattered thunderstorms are common all year long. According to the Red Cross, on average lightning kills ninety-three people and injures three hundred in the United States each year. If you hear thunder, you are close enough to be struck by lightning. Get off the water immediately. Seek a low-lying area without water. A good choice would be a sand dune field. Squat close to the ground with your hands on your knees and head between. Make yourself the smallest target possible. According to the NOAA, you should drop to the ground immediately if you feel an electric charge (hair standing on end or skin tingling), as lightning may be about ready to strike you. If someone is struck, call for help immediately if possible. According to Paul Auerbach in *Medicine for the Outdoors* (Elsevier, 2009), approximately two-thirds of those struck by lightning experience temporary paralysis called keraunoparalysis. This can result in cessation of breathing or cardiac arrest, therefore CPR may be necessary. Keep in mind that a radial pulse may not be present due to vasospasm after the strike. Cessation of breathing may last 15 to 30 minutes, according to Auerbach, so an apparently lifeless victim may be saved by rescue breathing promptly after the injury. Unless you witnessed the strike, assume that the person may have a head or spinal injury

from having been thrown some distance. The victim may be confused or unaware of having been struck by lightning and may be temporarily blind and/or deaf. First, second, or third degree burns may be present, but deep burns are rare and occur in less than 5 percent of cases.

Jellyfish and Siphonophores

The common jellyfish along the Texas coast are the lion's mane (*Cyanea capillata*), the sea nettle (*Chrysaora quinquecirrha*), moon jellyfish (*Aurelia aurita*), and cabbage head jellyfish (*Stomolophus meleagris*). Large numbers of moon jellyfish can be found in bays during midsummer. The sea nettle is another summer species and can be found in very low salinities in more estuarine bays. The lion's mane is by far the largest species found inshore. The bell in mature specimens in the western Gulf of Mexico can exceed 1 foot in diameter with several feet of tentacles armed with potent stinging nematocysts. The cabbage head jellyfish is primarily an offshore species that seasonally gets washed into bays, often in huge numbers in the late summer and fall. Kayaking through Aransas Pass in the fall I have seen so many that paddling through the huge clumps of jellyfish was difficult. Fortunately, this species is entirely harmless to humans. Although generally uncommon, the sea wasp (*Chiropsalmus quadramanus*) packs the most potent sting. It is more common in bays of higher salinity in the south and can occur in large numbers during years of drought.

The Portuguese man-of-war (*Physalia physalia*), also known as the bluebottle, is not a jellyfish but a siphonophore in the class Hydrozoa, recognizable by its small purple-blue float and proportionately long tentacles. It is an offshore, open ocean (pelagic) animal but often washes inshore. The specimens I have encountered and been stung by in Texas usually have a float less than 2 or 3 inches long and tentacles more than 6 feet long (unretracted). Specimens are often very common along the outer coast in the spring, especially after storms. Special care must be taken during surf launching and landings any time they are present on the beach or floating in the water (e.g., paddling jacket, gloves, wetsuit, and boots).

If you are entering or exiting the water and you feel an intense stinging pain and notice raised welts, you have probably been stung by a jellyfish. Do not rinse the affected area with fresh water because this may trigger more nematocysts (stinging cells) to discharge. If possible rinse the affected area with saline. Using sea water is possible but increases the risk for secondary infection later on. Isopropyl alcohol or a 5 percent solution of acetic acid (or vinegar) can be used to deactivate nematocysts. Large tentacles can be removed with forceps. Dr. Scott Plantz from the Department of Emergency Medicine at the Mount Sinai School of Medicine recommends using shaving cream after deactivating the nematocysts and gently shaving the affected area or scraping the area off with a knife to remove all foreign matter and stinging cells. If the sting is severe, it is wise to immobilize the patient to slow the spread of venom. Dr. Plantz also recommends a pressure-immobilization technique where the extremity (arm or leg) is wrapped tightly to decrease blood flow to the affected area but not cut off circulation. Hydrocortisone cream can be applied to the affected area two or three times a day but should be stopped if an infection becomes apparent. Keeping the affected area clean and applying Polysporin ointment twice a day is usually sufficient to prevent secondary infection.

Stingrays

Stingrays are flat-bodied fish that live in sandy areas where they often flap their bodies to disturb the sediment to expose clams, crabs, and other invertebrates on which they feed. Six species live in Texas waters,

Stingrays are common on the Texas coast and many injuries have resulted. However, these injuries can easily be avoided.

but only two are common in shallow nearshore waters: the Atlantic stingray (*Dasyatis sabina*) and the southern stingray (*D. americana*).

Neither is aggressive, but if stepped on they can use a venomous serrated spine to cause painful lacerations and puncture wounds that often become infected. All risk can be avoided simply by tapping the paddle on the bottom before exiting your boat and by shuffling your feet while in the water, causing stingrays to move away. If a person has been injured, Dr. Plantz recommends flushing the wound immediately with fresh water and then, for pain relief, soaking the affected area in water as hot as the patient can stand. The excruciating pain and increased bleeding usually peaks within one to two hours after the incident. Use tweezers to remove any remaining spines, scrub the wound with soap and water, and apply pressure to stop the bleeding. Immediate medical attention should be sought as oral antibiotics are indicated.

Oysters

Oysters, primarily *Crassostrea virginica,* are scattered throughout most Texas bays, especially on the north and central coast where river runoff is higher. In many places they form small islands and line bayside beaches. At low tide, winding ribbons of reef may be exposed. In some cases you may need to portage across a reef in order to get to a destination. These oysters are razor sharp. They can cut through thin neoprene boots and some shoes and can cause significant damage to composite hulls. Bacteria associated with the oysters can also cause infections. If a paddler has suffered a cut, it is important to wash the wound out with soap and water, disinfect it with Betadine (10 percent povidone-iodine) or alcohol, and use an antibiotic ointment two to three times a day.

Snakes

Four species of venomous snakes are seen on barrier islands and in coastal marshes: western cottonmouth (*Agkistrodon piscivorous leucostoma*); western diamondback (*Crotalus atrox*) and western massasauga (*Sistrurus catenatus tergeminus*) rattlesnakes; and coral snake (*Micrurus fulvius tenere*). The latter is uncommon and generally is found only on the northeastern Texas coast. The rattlesnakes are commonly reported, but I have seldom seen either. Joseph C. Britton and Brian Morton report in *Shore Ecology of the Gulf of Mexico* that they have commonly seen these snakes after tropical storms or hurricanes, when flooding forces them out of their burrows.

According to the Palm Beach Herpetological Society in cooperation with the University of Florida, there are some 15 fatalities each year from the 7,000 reported venomous snake bites in the United States. Of these, more than 3,000 involve the victim inappropriately handling a snake. More than 85 percent of bites are below the knee, and in half of cases involving rattlesnakes and other pit vipers, no venom is injected because strikes against humans are often defensive.

The amount of venom injected by a coral snake is proportionate to the size of the snake and the length of time it holds onto its victim. A coral snake bite generally involves little pain, and it is best to pull the snake off immediately as the fangs are small and the snake has to work to get the venom into the victim. Depending on the amount of venom received, onset of signs and symptoms may take up to twelve hours. Victims may experience drowsiness, slurred speech, and tremors. Severe cases may result in respiratory arrest and cardiac failure.

A pit viper bite produces two distinct puncture wounds with intense, burning pain and swelling proportional to the amount of venom injected. Victims may experience tingling, nausea, and vomiting. Again respiratory arrest and cardiac failure may result in severe cases.

Some commercial suction devices have been shown to remove significant amounts of venom without incision if used immediately after a bite. Clean the wound thoroughly with soap and water and apply a sterile dressing. Wrap a bandage about two to four inches above the bite to restrict blood flow but not cut off circulation. Do not use a tourniquet, as this isolates the venom and concentrates damage from enzymes. Remove all rings and watches and keep the affected limb below the heart. Apply a splint to help immobilize the limb if possible. Swelling is the major indica-

tor of how much venom was received by the victim. Relax and avoid panic; chances of survival are 499 out of 500. Do nothing to increase heart rate or peripheral blood flow (e.g., exercise such as running or paddling, or drinking alcohol). Do not cut the wound. This causes more damage than benefit. Positively identify the snake if possible. Seek immediate medical treatment to obtain anti-venom and a tetanus shot.

Sun and Heat

Just like waves in the sea, colors in the visible light spectrum vary by wavelength (400–750 nm), and their intensity varies by the square of the wave height or amplitude. Colors vary from the shorter violet to longer red wavelengths. Bending wavelengths of light is called refraction. Shorter wavelengths are more easily refracted and are scattered more easily by the atmosphere than are longer wavelengths. For example, more of the shorter wavelengths are scattered or filtered out at sunrise and sunset because the light is traveling at an oblique angle through more of the atmosphere. This is why we have those beautiful orange and red sunsets. Shorter wavelengths scattered in the atmosphere at midday make the sky appear blue at sea level. Shorter wavelengths are also more easily scattered and reflected off the surface of bodies of water. This is why oceans and lakes appear blue at a distance. These differences in the refractive indices of light within the visual spectrum allow spherical water droplets in the atmosphere to disperse white light into a rainbow. The less easily "bent" or refracted long wavelength red is always on the top of the rainbow, while shorter wavelength violet and blue are underneath along the bottom.

Shorter wavelength ultraviolet (UV) light is just below the visible spectrum (290–400 nm) and is responsible for sunburn. These rays of light are even more easily scattered than visible blue or violet light. This is why it is easier to become severely burned on the water. Also, UV light penetrates wet skin more easily than dry, and limbs are more susceptible to burns than the face, neck, and trunk. Because UV light is even more easily filtered out by the atmosphere than the short wavelengths in the visible spectrum, about 65 percent of all incident UV light reaches us during the four hours between 10:00 A.M. and 2:00 P.M. People with blond or red hair and blue eyes are at greatest risk for sunburns. Compared to fair-skinned people, those with moderately pigmented skin can tolerate 3–5 times more UV exposure, while African Americans can tolerate up to 30 times more UV exposure. (Those who go to tanning beds increase their tolerance to UV exposure by only 2–3 times.)

At the end of the day, if the skin feels warm and is tender, red, and swollen, then you have been burned. If blistering occurs, second degree burns may have been sustained. In these cases it is important to prevent further exposure, keep the person well hydrated, and seek medical attention. For the rest of us analgesics such as aspirin and acetaminophen and nonsteroidal anti-inflammatory drugs like ibuprofen may help relieve pain and inflammation. The latter usually peaks within twenty-four hours. Although systemic steroids when given early and in large doses may be helpful, topical steroids have been shown to have little if any benefit.

Sunburn can ruin a trip. To avoid it, hats, sunglasses, and sunscreen are recommended. Since the coast is often windy, I have found wide-brimmed hats difficult to wear. Many paddlers prefer a billed hat with a fabric cape that protects the ears and neck. There is no substitute for polarized glasses. A good polarized lens screens out harmful rays, increases contrast, and decreases glare off the water. Frames should be swept or form fitting to protect the eye from incident light coming in from the sides, but not so tight as to restrict air flow around the eyes, which could cause fogging. Oakley produces a one-piece frame for prescription lenses with vents that prevent fogging on the back lens surface and a head strap that prevents the glasses from coming off even in heavy surf or when rolling a boat. The product also comes with an anti-fog solution to rub onto the lenses. Some sports frames have specialized adjustable nose pieces and temples to adjust air flow. Waterproof sunscreen lotions and sprays of SPF 30 or greater are recommended and should be used liberally. Some of these also contain N,N-Diethyl-m-toluamide (DEET) to repel mosquitoes; this can be convenient when traveling through the bays, especially in the north, where there are generally more mosquitoes because of higher rainfall and freshwater runoff.

Dehydration, heat exhaustion, and sunstroke (hyperpyrexia) are also of concern, especially during the hotter months along the Texas coast, where there is little or no shade, fresh water can be hard to find, and medical attention may not be quickly available. Endurance athletes paddling the coast should take care not to confuse heat exhaustion with hyponatremia from electrolyte imbalance. There is extensive information on these conditions in books and online. Paddlers deciding to visit the Texas coast to kayak during the hotter months should be familiar with the signs, symptoms, and treatment of both conditions. People from more northern climates are not acclimated to heat and humidity and should be especially wary. Prevention is the best way to avoid these conditions. Following are tips for kayakers:

(1) Drink plenty of fluids, but avoid carbonated and caffeinated drinks. Bring sports drinks or powdered mixes that can be used to maintain electrolyte balance. During most of the year one gallon of water per person per day is acceptable, but during the hotter months more is necessary. I prefer to bring powdered drink mixes along with my water to mix as necessary.

Shell beaches in the bays provide a durable surface for camping and can minimize the effect of campers on these shorelines. Photo by Ken Johnson

◄ *Leave-no-trace principles should be followed when camping along the shore. Photo by Ken Johnson*

▲ *Those embarking on multiday trips should be prepared with food, water, and essential equipment in dry bags. This may include a weather radio, GPS receiver, compass, maps, cell phone, VHF radio, flashlight, headlamp, cookware, matches, fire starter, sunscreen, extra clothing, duct tape, a repair kit for your boats, and a windproof tent with stakes appropriate for sand and shell beaches.*

(2) Splash yourself with water to keep cool. Learn to lower yourself into the water off the bow of another boat or simply roll the boat to cool off. Dipping your hat in the water is a good way to keep your head cooler. Soaking the neoprene deck of a spray skirt can also help keep you cool.

(3) Stay out of the bays during the hottest months, especially when there is little wind. Usually on the outer coast, the wind blowing in off the water has a tremendous cooling effect. During the late morning and early afternoon, I like to use driftwood or paddles to suspend a tarp or tent fly to provide shade on the beach for lunch and for a short siesta sheltered from the sun.

Camping

Most of the designated camping areas listed in this book are primitive, without water or facilities of any kind. Minimize your impact on these areas as much as possible and always carry out what you carried in. Try to use stoves and do not burn campfires unless there are designated fire pits at established campsites. Great care should be taken to obey the rules for camping within the jurisdiction of the Padre Island National Seashore and state and county parks. It may be necessary to obtain permission to camp from private landholders in some places along the coast. Specific details on whom to contact for permission and any additional requirements and information are provided in the trip description section of this book. If camping on a spoil island along the intracoastal waterway, make sure there are no signs declaring the island a bird nesting sanctuary, and respect private property when small hunting and fishing shacks are present.

Kayaking Resources

The establishments in the list that follows can provide information on local clubs, kayak instruction, equipment, rentals, and outfitting:

Austin Canoe and Kayak, 9705 Burnet Rd #102, Austin, TX 78758, 512-719-4386, www.austinkayak.com

Austin Canoe and Kayak, 4554 S IH 35, San Marcos, TX 78666, 512-396-2386, www.austinkayak.com

Austin Canoe and Kayak, 5822 Bissonnet, Houston, TX 77081, 713-660-7000, www.austinkayak.com

Canoesport, 5808 South Rice Avenue, Houston, TX 77081, 713-660-7000, www.canoesport.com

Corpus Christi Kayak Tours and Rentals, Corpus Christi, TX, 361-855-3926, http://home.earthlink.net/~johnsonkw/kayak-corpus/

High Trails, 3610 Marquis Drive, Garland, TX 75042, 972-272-3353, www.hightrailscanoe.com

Kayak Power, Training and Rentals, Dallas, 214-669-1663, www.KayakPower.com

Mountain Sports, Hwy 39 West, Hunt, TX 78024, 830-238-4400, www.quintanna.com/mtnsports

OKC Kayak, 220 N. Western Ave., Oklahoma City, OK 73106, 405-830-9689, www.okckayak.com

REI—Austin, 9901 North Capitol of Texas Hwy, Austin, TX 78759, 512-343-5550, www.rei.com/stores/austin

REI—Dallas, 4515 LBJ Freeway, Dallas, TX 75244, 972-490-5989, www.rei.com/stores/dallas

REI—Houston, 7538 Westheimer Road, Houston, TX 77063, 713-353-2582, www.rei.com/stores/houston

Rockport Kayak Outfitters, 106 South Austin Street, Rockport, TX 78382, 361-729-1505 or 866-729-1505, www.captainsally.com

Southwest Paddle Sports, 26322 I-45 North, The Woodlands, Houston, Texas 77386–1022, 281-292-5600, www.paddlesports.com

Guidebooks

Books giving information on the biology, ecology, parks, and history of the Texas coast can enrich any paddler's journey. Some of the selections that follow are out of print but copies may nevertheless be available.

Jean Andrews, *Texas Shells: A Field Guide,* Elma Dill Russell Spencer Foundation Series (Austin: University of Texas Press, 1981)

Jim Blackburn, *The Book of Texas Bays* (College Station: Texas A&M University Press, 2004)

Joseph C. Britton and Brian Morton, *Shore Ecology of the Gulf of Mexico* (Austin: University of Texas Press, 1989)

Mary Michael Cannatella and Rita Arnold, *Plants of the Texas Shore: A Beachcomber's Guide* (College Station: Texas A&M University Press, 1985)

James R. Dixon, *Amphibians and Reptiles of Texas,* 2nd edition (College Station: Texas A&M University Press, 2000)

William C. Foster, ed., *The La Salle Expedition in Texas: The Journal of Henri Joutel, 1684–1687* (Denton: Texas State Historical Association, 1998)

John Graves, *Goodbye to a River* (New York: Alfred A. Knopf, 1960)

Stephan L. Hatch, Joseph L. Schuster, and D. Lynn Drawe, *Grasses of the Texas Gulf Prairies and Marshes,* W. L. Moody Jr. Natural History Series no. 24 (College Station: Texas A&M University Press, 1999)

Larry D. Hodge, *Official Guide to Texas Wildlife Management Areas* (Austin: University of Texas Press, 2001)

H. Dickson Hoese, and Richard H. Moore, *Fishes of the Gulf of Mexico: Texas, Louisiana, and Adjacent*

Landing and camping are not allowed on islands that serve as bird rookeries. Photo by Ken Johnson

Waters, W. L. Moody Jr. Natural History Series no. 22 (College Station: Texas A&M University Press, 1998)

Erik Larson, *Isaac's Storm: A Man, a Time and the Deadliest Hurricane in History* (New York: Vantage Press, 2000)

Roy L. Lehman, Ruth O'Brien, and Tammy White, *Plants of the Texas Coastal Bend* (College Station: Texas A&M University Press, 2005)

Wayne H. McAlister and Martha K. McAlister, *Aransas: A Naturalist's Guide* (Austin: University of Texas Press, 1995)

——, *Guidebook to the Aransas National Wildlife Refuge* (Victoria, Tex.: Mince Country Press, 1987)

——, *Life on Matagorda Island* (College Station: Texas A&M University Press, 2004)

——, *Matagorda Island, A Naturalist's Guide* (Austin: University of Texas Press, 1992)

David G. McComb, *The Historic Seacoast of Texas* (Austin: University of Texas Press, 1999)

John H. Rappole and Gene W. Blacklock, *Birds of Texas: A Field Guide,* W. L. Moody Jr. Natural History Series no. 14 (College Station: Texas A&M University Press, 1994)

K. D. Reese, *Boats n' Blinds an' Other Fascinatin' Tales* (Victoria, Tex.: Salt Grass Press, 2001)

Alfred Richardson, *Wildflowers and Other Plants of Texas Beaches and Islands* (Austin: University of Texas Press, 2002)

Phil H. Shook, Chuck Scates, and David Sams, *Fly Fishing the Texas Coast: Backcountry Flats to Bluewater* (Boulder, Colo.: Pruett Publishing Company, 1999)

Robert R. Stickney, *Estuarine Ecology of the Southeastern United States and Gulf of Mexico,* 1st edition (College Station: Texas A&M University Press, 1984)

Robert S. Weddle, *The Wreck of the Belle: The Ruin of La Salle* (College Station: Texas A&M University Press, 2001)

Bonnie R. Weise and William A. White, *Padre Island National Seashore: A Guide to the Geology, Natural Environments, and History of a Texas Barrier Island* (Austin: Bureau of Economic Geology, University of Texas, 1980)

John S. Whorff, "Paddling the Central Texas Coast," *Sea Kayaker Magazine* 16, no. 5 (1999): 18–25

J. S. Whorff, L. L. Whorff, and M. H. Sweet, "Spatial Variation in an Algal Turf Community with Respect to Substratum Slope and Wave Height," *Journal of the Marine Biological Association of the United Kingdom* 75 (1995): 429–44

Linda Wolff, *Indianola and Matagorda Island, 1837–1887: A Local History and Visitor's Guide for a Lost Seaport and a Barrier Island on the Texas Gulf Coast* (Austin: Eakin Press, 1999)

Bernd Wursig, Thomas A. Jefferson, and David J. Schmidly, *The Marine Mammals of the Gulf of Mexico* (College Station: Texas A&M University Press, 2000)

How to Use This Book

Coastal overview key showing major bays and passes along the Texas coast: 1 = Galveston Bay and barrier island complex, 2 = Bryan Beach to Matagorda Bay, 3 = Matagorda Bay to San Antonio Bay, 4 = Goose Island State Park and Aransas National Wildlife Refuge, 5 = Aransas Bay and vicinity, 6 = Corpus Christi Bay, 7 = Padre Island National Seashore, 8 = Baffin Bay, 9 = Port Mansfield, 10 = Boca Chica State Park/Isla Blanca County Park.

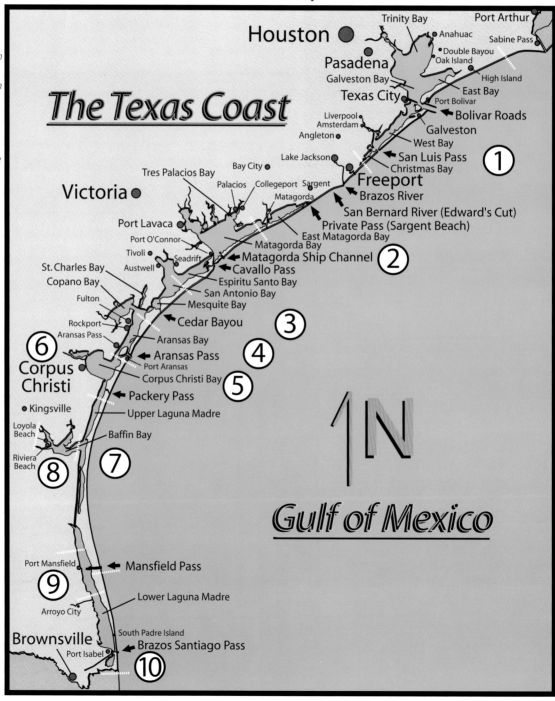

Routes are divided into ten sections based on geography and information content (see key map). The Galveston Bay and barrier island complex is so large that I opted to divide it into eastern and western sections. Some areas of the coast have been omitted because of access and/or pollution problems.

Each section opens with an introduction giving pertinent information regarding wildlife and coastal physical and cultural geography. The introduction is followed by information on:

- Recommended Navigational Aids
- Planning Considerations
- Accommodations
- Directions to Launch Sites

Side trips are suggested in some places.

Maps and route descriptions follow, with distances and level of expertise given at the beginning of each route description. The distances were determined using navigational charts, scaled aerial images, and GPS or a combination of these. Distances are given in statute miles because people are generally more familiar with this unit of measure and often underestimate distances using nautical miles.

The level of expertise required to paddle a route safely is rated as "beginning," "intermediate," or "advanced." These are arguably subjective terms, but the definitions in this book are as follows:

"Beginning" means routes in generally calm water over short distances in shallow water without any open water crossings. This level does not require special navigational skills and overnight camping preparation.

"Intermediate" refers to routes over longer distances that may include open water crossings and moderately choppy water without breaking waves. It requires basic navigational expertise, good camping skills and some degree of fitness.

"Advanced" refers to routes which may be long, in rough water or with long open water crossings that require physical fitness and good navigational and camping skills. However, these designations are not absolute and are no replacement for good judgment, discipline and common sense.

Any of these routes can change designation depending on environmental conditions. Remember: **KAYAKING CAN BE DANGEROUS**. If you are not trained and prepared, and do not have proper equipment, then do not attempt these routes. Note that the maps included are not intended to replace the navigational aids recommended in each section.

PART 2

KAYAKING ROUTES

Galveston Barrier Island and Bay Complex

THE GALVESTON BARRIER ISLAND AND BAY Complex is located along the northeast coast extending from just north of Freeport to High Island and including Follet's Island, Galveston Island, the Bolivar Peninsula, and all embayments and bayous to the west and north. This complex forms the largest estuary system along the Texas coast and the seventh largest in the United States. From Freeport to Sabine Pass, extensive intertidal marshes line estuarine bayshores to a greater extent than anywhere else along the coast. Britton and Morton (1989) note that these marshes tend to diminish south of Freeport. Bayshore vegetation profiles reported at Drum Bay and Galveston Island State Park show that mixed stands of two species of cordgrass (*Spartina patens* and *S. alterniflora*) dominate a band of 300 feet or more of tidal flats along the shoreline. These stands help trap sediment, prevent shoreline erosion, and provide refuge and food for a variety of wildlife. Trapping sediments also helps decrease turbidity that can smother oyster reefs and kill sea grass beds. Salt marshes are important nursery grounds for a variety of juvenile fish, crabs, and shrimp because they provide refuge and a rich food supply. During the 1980s nearshore waters and the Galveston Bay complex accounted for approximately a third of the shrimp and blue crab catch and nearly two-thirds of the oyster harvest in the state of Texas. Hundreds of resident and migrant bird species have been reported along these bayshores and utilize small islands, oyster reefs, salt marshes, tidal flats, and shallow bays for food and refuge from predators.

The bay area is a center for shipping and petrochemical industry and, with about 4.8 million people, has been heavily impacted by industrial and municipal development. In fact, the shipping tonnage passing through the Port of Houston ranks number two and the Port of Galveston number twelve in the United States. Much of the original bayshore habitat has been destroyed by significant erosion and shoreline subsidence caused by boat traffic on bays and the intracoastal waterway and, in places, by withdrawal of groundwater. In addition, increased turbidity from boat traffic and dredging activities have contributed to killing sea grass beds and oyster reefs, resulting in declining fishery stocks. Other threats to submerged vegetation include uprooting by boats, trampling by wade fisherman, and raw sewage from fishing and hunting cabins.

Despite these serious environmental problems, coastal prairies and salt marshes have been preserved along some of the bays, and many restoration projects have been carried out or are soon to be undertaken. The Christmas Bay Coastal Preserve is a great example and a good place for kayakers to visit. The preserve supports rich marshland and extensive oyster reefs. Its sea grass beds represent some of the few remaining in the entire Galveston Bay area. These beds consist primarily of shoalgrass (*Halodule wrightii*), turtlegrass (*Thalassia testudinum*), and clovergrass (*Halophila engelmanii*). Widgeongrass (*Ruppia maritima*) is another submerged aquatic plant found in these beds and scattered throughout Galveston Bay. Due to its importance to waterfowl, much information is available on the establishment and management of widgeongrass, which has been useful in bay restoration projects.

Multiagency habitat restoration projects are under way in an attempt to recover some of what has been lost. The paddling trails that showcase efforts to enhance marsh habitat and sea grass beds along the bayshore at Galveston Island State Park are a good example. Sand-filled geotextile tubes have been used to create a matrix of terraces and to dampen wave action, preventing shoreline subsidence and erosion. Smooth and marsh hay cordgrass were planted on the terraces to protect them from erosion and to provide habitat for birds, shrimp, crabs, and small fish. This project involved the efforts of personnel from the Texas Parks and Wildlife Department, U.S. Fish and Wildlife Service, Texas General Land Office, Galveston Bay Foundation, the U.S Army Corps of Engineers, and an environmental engineering/consulting firm.

Paddlers can see beautiful riparian hardwood forests that still transect some coastal prairies despite encroaching development. Examples of the latter include Chocolate and Armand bayous, where live oak, water oak, magnolia, hackberry, and other trees grow along the waterways. One of the few remnants of Texas coastal prairie can be seen at the Armand Bayou Nature Center and the Brazoria National Wildlife Refuge. Unfortunately, some of the areas in and adjacent to the Brazoria refuge have been used for ranching and rice farming, resulting in channelization and altered hydrology. In addition, exotic species such as the Chinese tallow tree have invaded the area. Current management and restoration plans may also help these areas to recover. Armand Bayou Nature Center provides excellent insight into the bayou systems of Galveston Bay and the upper Texas coast. One of the interesting things I learned at the center was that the American bison, our largest land mammal, once roamed these coastal prairies in large numbers. Fossil bones have been found along the Texas coast that date back more than 35,000 years. Armand Bayou is home to a large alligator population. In fact, this may be the easiest place for paddlers to observe them. When paddling around alligators be cautious and keep a safe distance so as not to disturb them. Paddling along this bayou I have also seen a wide array of birds and different vegetation types.

Kayakers should be wary of jagged oyster reefs, especially in primary bays. Oyster reefs consisting primarily of *Crassostrea virginica* are prolific in the less disturbed and polluted bay systems because periodic freshwater runoff can drop salinity to less than a third that of normal sea water, killing many of the oysters' parasites, competitors, and predators. However, some researchers like Eric Powell from Texas A&M suggest that oyster reefs can prosper in higher average salinities when significant currents and abundant food are available. Although there is generally less diversity of marine animals and algae on these reefs when compared to the central Texas coast, there is often much greater abundance of those species that can survive because of the high primary productivity from the extensive salt marshes. However, pollution and sedimentation from dredging activities, storms, and floods have taken their toll on oyster populations in general on the north coast.

Increasing wildlife habitat destruction and pollution from development (agricultural, industrial, and residential) led to the formulation and implementation of the Galveston Bay Plan, a twenty-year plan to help restore this bay system (http://gbic.tamug.edu/theplan .html). Although the plan was implemented in 1995, the foundation of the effort began with the establishment of the Galveston Bay Estuary Program in 1989 by the Environmental Protection Agency. The science-based program is administered by the Texas Commission on Environmental Quality (TCEQ) and coordinates efforts by government agencies, universities, conservation organizations, businesses, industry, and citizens who are interested in protecting and restoring this bay system. I am optimistic that continued plans will help restore this bay system to a more natural state. For more detailed information on the current state of the bay system, contact the Galveston Bay Information Center (gbic.tamug. edu/index.html).

For the purposes of this book, the barrier island and bay complex is divided into two parts, east and west. The East Galveston Bay section is focused on the Bolivar Peninsula and kayak routes on bays and bayous behind it. The West Galveston Bay section includes Follet's Island and Galveston Island and kayak routes on bays and bayous behind them.

East Galveston Bay Complex

This section encompasses selected kayak routes from the Bolivar Peninsula to the myriad of lakes and bayous associated with the Trinity River delta system. The Bolivar Peninsula forms a long sandy spit that flanks East Bay for more than 25 miles. The peninsula extends southwest toward Galveston and Pelican Island and at its southern tip are 4.5 miles of jetty that form the north side of the ship channel entering Galveston Bay, referred to as Bolivar Roads. The Houston Audubon

Society manages three bird sanctuaries on the Bolivar Peninsula: Horseshoe Marsh and Bolivar Flats at the south end of the peninsula and Mundy Marsh near Gilchrist. These sanctuaries provide significant nesting habitat and are critically important to birds migrating north from Central and South America. People come from all over the country to observe birds on the peninsula, especially during the spring migration. Behind the peninsula is the protected Gulf Intracoastal Waterway used to move barges up and down the busy Texas coast. In addition, many commercial fishermen are based on the Bolivar Peninsula. For paddlers, this is a great place to observe seaborne commerce.

The Bolivar Peninsula was named by Warren Hall and Henry Perry in 1815 for famed South American general and president Simon Bolívar. In the early 1800s the peninsula was used by pirates like Michael Aury to transport slaves between Galveston and Louisiana. About 1816 some Spanish explorers built an earthen levee to protect themselves and their men from Karankawa Indians. Dr. James Long built Fort Las Casas on the same site in 1820 while preparing to attack Presidio de Bahia around present day Goliad. The primitive stronghold was renamed Fort Green during the Civil War. The present Fort Travis was built on the same site and was completed in 1899, the year before the Galveston hurricane. After the storm, the fort was rebuilt with 15-foot seawalls. In 1942 the garrison was expanded to accommodate 2,500 troops and many gun emplacements were added, including antiaircraft batteries. Paddlers can camp at the old decommissioned fort, which is now run by the Galveston County Parks Department. This park is well worth a visit.

The original Bolivar Lighthouse was built in 1852 and torn down during the Civil War. A temporary lighthouse made of wood was erected in its place in 1865. The current lighthouse was built in 1872 with brick and sheathed in iron plates riveted together to withstand the elements. Local residents sought refuge in the 117-foot-tall lighthouse during the 1900 and 1915 hurricanes and survived. This lighthouse still provides a good landmark for paddlers around the peninsula.

East Bay is separated from Trinity Bay to the north by a tongue of land culminating at Smith Point.

Double Bayou empties into the east side of Trinity Bay and forks into twin arms that wind inland for miles. There are working fishing boats here as well as a few boat wrecks along middle of the east fork. Often hundreds of giant webs are spun across the bayou by banana spiders (*Nephila clavipes*), and platter-sized turtles and sea monster-sized alligator gar (*Atractosteus spatula*) swim in the waters below. These fish may weigh in at more than 350 pounds. Paddling from Trinity Bay to Double Bayou Park is an experience to remember.

The north end of Trinity Bay is dominated by the Trinity River delta with its maze of alligator-filled bayous, lakes, and tertiary embayments. Cotton Lake, Lake Anahuac, Jack's Pass, and White's Bayous are examples. Overlooking Lake Anahuac and the Trinity River delta is the town of Anahuac, home of the annual Gatorfest and appropriately designated by the state legislature as the alligator capital of Texas! Fort Anahuac Park on the south side of town is now a good place for kayakers to launch, land, and picnic.

Large stands of the bald cypress (*Taxodium distichum*) flourish in the nutrient-rich waters of the northern Trinity River delta, especially around Mud and Miller lakes and Lake Charlotte. With their huge buttressed trunks and extensive prop root "knees" trapping the rich sediment, cypress trees are said to grow larger than any other tree east of the Rocky Mountains. Bald cypress can exceed 140 feet in height and 17 feet in diameter at the base. Along the shoreline are shell beaches littered with the marsh clam (*Rangia cuneata*). These clams were a large part of the diet of the Indians inhabiting the lower Trinity basin. Paddling through these forests and the plethora of vegetation can be compared with touring a botanical garden and is an ethereal experience reserved for paddlers alone. Motorized boats are prohibited from launching at Cedar Hill Park, the only launching area on Lake Charlotte. Along the southwestern shore of Miller Lake is a large berm where paddlers can rest. This berm was once the site of an old Indian village and French trading post established by Joseph Blancpain in 1754.

Overall this section offers paddlers views of maritime commerce, a historic lighthouse, old forts, bayous, cypress forests, marsh clam beaches, world class birding, and extensive wildlife somewhat different than the rest of the coast. It seems ironic that many of these destinations feel so remote and yet are so close to the millions of people living in the greater Houston area.

Recommended Navigational Aids

Boater's Map of Galveston Bay Area (With GPS) and *Wade Fishing Map of East Galveston Bay Area (With GPS)* by Hook-N-Line Map Company; aerial maps downloaded from TerraServer (www.terraserver.com), Google Earth (http://earth.google.com), or MapQuest (www.mapquest.com).

Planning Considerations

If you are riding on the Galveston Island Ferry to Port Bolivar, be aware that on busy weekends it may take several hours of waiting in line to cross. During these times it is wise to cross early in the morning or late at night. If you cannot avoid peak hours, it may be wise to drive around the east side of the peninsula through High Island and avoid the ferry altogether. The water is shallow and there are extensive oyster reefs at Bolivar Flats; kayakers should avoid paddling in this area during low tides or when the wind is blowing strongly out of the north. If you are kayaking along the intracoastal waterway on the north side of Bolivar Peninsula, avoid boat traffic and stay out of the middle of the waterway. For paddling the bayous of the Trinity River delta west of Anahuac or around Lake Charlotte, GPS, a compass, and good maps are essential. Getting lost is easy and can be dangerous in these areas.

For most emergencies, a VHF radio or a cell phone is adequate. If calling from your cell phone, the Galveston Coast Guard Station number is 409-766-5633. For emergencies, dial 911 or call the Chambers County sheriff at 409-267-8322 and in Galveston County call 409-766-2322.

Accommodations

To stay at historic Fort Travis Park on the Bolivar Peninsula, camp sites are $20 per night and cabanas are $25 per night. Restrooms are nearby. For information call the Galveston County Parks Department at 409-934-8100 or for reservations call 409-934-8126. Food

and lodging are available at nearby Crystal Beach (www.crystalbeach.com), although Hurricane Ike destroyed many businesses. For those visiting Anahuac, there are few restaurants and the nearest lodging is 18 miles east in the town of Winnie (www.winnietexas.org). Camping with showers is available at Fort Anahuac Park, and camping without showers is available at Cedar Hill Park along Lake Charlotte. Permits must be obtained ahead of time through the Chambers County Parks Department in Anahuac (www.co.chambers.tx.us/offices/parks.html, 409-267-3041).

Directions to Launch Sites

Bolivar Peninsula: From Houston, travel south on Interstate 45 across the causeway to Galveston. Follow Avenue J or Broadway Street and turn left on Seawall Boulevard. Continue northeast on Seawall Boulevard and turn left on Ferry Road to get to the Galveston Island Ferry that crosses Bolivar Roads to get to Port Bolivar. Alternatively, drive west on Interstate 10 to Highway 124 and drive south through High Island to turn right on Highway 87 down the Bolivar Peninsula. To get to Pilsner boat ramp drive from the ferry terminal past the Bolivar Lighthouse and Fort Travis and turn right on 16th Street. Park on the beach near the boat ramp. The Bolivar Flats access is from the north jetty at the end of 17th Street, one block farther north. To get to the beach launch area on the west end of Horseshoe Marsh Bird Sanctuary, turn left off Highway 87 on French Town Road almost immediately after getting off the ferry. Drive north and you will see Horseshoe Lake with extensive oyster reefs. Across the lake you will also see the Bolivar Lighthouse. Just before the bridge across the mouth of Horseshoe Lake, the beach where you can park and launch is on your left.

Double Bayou: The two popular access points are at Job Beason Park in the small town of Oak Island and at Double Bayou Park near the small town of Double Bayou. To get to Beason Park, drive east from Houston on Interstate 10. Turn south on FM 563 and drive past Lake Anahuac and the town of Anahuac. You will see that 563 becomes Eagle Road. Continue south and the road takes three 90-degree turns (right, left, right) and comes west into the small town of Oak Island. Turn left on West Bayshore Road and follow it through two more right-angle turns (right, left) to reach the Beason Park boat ramp and parking area. To get to Double Bayou Park, take Interstate 10 east from Houston and turn south on Highway 61. After 4 miles, the road turns into FM 562; 11 miles south of Interstate 10, just past the small town of Double Bayou, turn right on Eagle Ferry Road. The park is on the left about 0.4 mile from the intersection. Drive to the back of the park to get to the boat ramp on the bayou.

Fort Anahuac Park: Drive east from Houston on Interstate 10 and turn south on FM 563. Drive past Lake Anahuac to the town of Anahuac. Turn right off FM 563 on Belton Lane and then turn left on South Main Street. The park is on your right. Drive toward the back of the park, down the bluff, and along a small embayment to the parking area and boat ramp to launch through a channel into the Trinity River. Boats can also launch from the shore along the road south of the parking area and boat ramp.

White Memorial Park: Drive east from Houston on Interstate 10 and turn south on Highway 61. Take the first right south of the highway access road on White Park Road and drive west. As the road begins to turn south, turn right on the dirt road to the parking area and boat ramp on the bayou. There is a nice place to put in along the shore to the left of the boat ramp on White Bayou.

Cedar Hill Park: To access Lake Charlotte, drive east of Houston on Interstate 10 and turn north on FM 563. Follow the road north past Sherman Road and turn left on Lake Charlotte Road. WARNING: this road is easy to miss. If you enter Liberty County or pass County Road 125, you have gone too far. Drive east on Lake Charlotte Road for about a mile and you will see the Sherman Cemetery on the right. The park entrance is on the left across the street from the cemetery; at the time of writing there was no sign for the park. Drive to the back of the park, where there is a place for paddlers to launch on Lake Charlotte. The traditional put-in is on Trinity River, but the Interstate 10 access road has not been accessible because of construction for several years and is not nearly as nice as Cedar Hill Park.

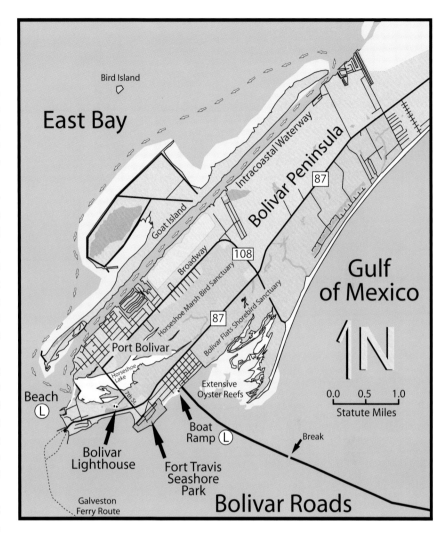

The southern end of the Bolivar Peninsula. Arrows mark the Goat Island circumnavigation and L indicates launch sites.

Fort Travis and the North Jetty

INTERMEDIATE TO ADVANCED

variable mileage

Launch at the Pilsner boat ramp or the adjacent beach. There is a restroom with shower here. Paddle around the seawalls of Fort Travis and down the Bolivar Roads side of the jetty. There is often very good fishing here along the rocks and jetty blocks. The area can be rough. One fun thing to do is paddle out along the jetty approximately 1.6 miles and pass through the break in the jetty to Bolivar Flats. You can land along the north jetty, but beware of low water and oysters.

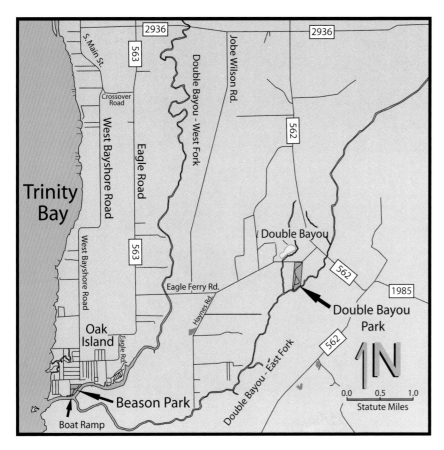

The east and west forks of Double Bayou along Trinity Bay. Most paddlers launch from the public boat ramp at Beason Park and paddle the east fork to Double Bayou Park.

Bolivar Flats

INTERMEDIATE

variable mileage

Launch from the north jetty access and paddle right offshore around the Bolivar Flats to go birdwatching. This is one of the best places to watch birds on the entire north coast. However, beware of oysters and shallow water related to north winds and low tides. When I first paddled this area in 1989, the flats were far less prominent than they are now, and the area was badly polluted. As suggested for Fort Travis, you can paddle about 1.6 miles down the jetty to the break and paddle back on the other side to land on the beach or at the Pilsner boat ramp, which has a restroom and shower.

Goat Island Circumnavigation

INTERMEDIATE

11.4 miles

The beach adjacent to Horseshoe Lake is beautiful. Walk up the beach face and look over Horseshoe Lake and you usually see large numbers of birds along extensive oyster reefs, with the Bolivar Lighthouse visible beyond the lake. The structure provides an excellent landmark for paddlers. Launch from the beach and paddle north into the intracoastal waterway. Slower paddlers do not belong here, as it is important to be able to get out of the way of boat traffic, including barges and commercial fishing boats. As you paddle northeast along the intracoastal, you will see barges waiting in line to cross or enter Bolivar Roads and the small commercial fishing fleet loading, unloading, and refitting boats. Beautiful homes are being built along the waterway. You will notice on maps that all the islands behind the Bolivar Peninsula flanking the intracoastal waterway are referred to as "Goat Island." A little less than 5 miles down the waterway is the end of the first Goat Island. On your right you will see the Bolivar Yacht Basin. Food and bait can be obtained here. A good rest stop can also be found along the beach toward the end of Goat Island. However, be careful to pull your boat high on the shore or you may have it washed out into the channel by a barge! Paddle north into East Bay to continue. You will wonder if you can really circumnavigate the island as the water is so shallow. Paddle out into the bay if it is too shallow. Following the back of the island southwest, stay somewhat offshore to avoid extremely shallow water. The shoreline juts out in front of you. As you get closer, you may see some white geotextile tubes filled with sand that are being used to retard erosion here. As you turn around the island to go south, you will see an inlet to your left. This is not the opening to the intracoastal waterway. When I first did this route, I had 1995 aerial maps and this feature did not exist back then. Continue following the shoreline, and. you will see the lighthouse and beach as you round the end of the island.

Double Bayou

INTERMEDIATE

5 miles Beason Park to Double Bayou Park, 10 miles roundtrip

Launch from Beason Park in the small town of Oak Island. Since both branches of Double Bayou are relatively deep, sailboats from Houston are often seen here and it is a popular overnight destination, according to the Houston Canoe Club. Paddle into the right or east branch of Double Bayou. On my last trip here we saw several small alligators and the largest alligator gar I have ever seen. These fish can live for more than 75 years, attain lengths in excess of 9 feet, and weigh more than 300 pounds! Another interesting sight was hundreds of colorful banana spiders suspended in thick webs above the bayou. Near a fishing boat wreck in the bayou, I pointed my camera upward and captured more than 20 fist-sized spiders in the image. After about 5 miles you reach the boat ramp at the edge of Double Bayou Park on your left. The park has picnic tables suitable for lunch, a poorly maintained restroom, and a covered pavilion. Return to Beason Park to finish this interesting trip. An interesting side trip is to the small island in Trinity Bay at the mouth of Double Bayou. The island is half a mile from the launch site at Beason Park, or one mile roundtrip. If doing a one-way trip, it is easier to start from Double Bayou Park.

▲ *The Beason Park boat ramp next to Pirates Landing is a popular place to access Double Bayou.*

▼ *Large banana spiders with webs spanning Double Bayou are a common sight; they are also known as golden orb-weaver spiders (Nephila clavipes). The much larger female in this picture was in excess of three inches in size and may represent a poorly known subspecies.*

▼ *Many trees form canopies over Double Bayou, making for a quiet and shady paddling experience.*

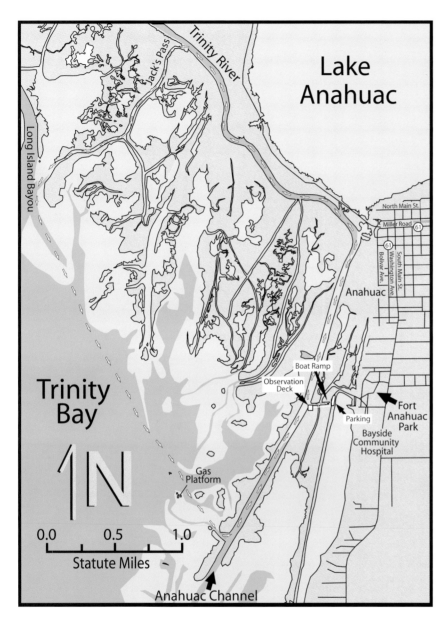

Fort Anahuac Park
along the Trinity River
delta. Arrows denote
the Trinity River delta
loop.

the Trinity River and turn north. Paddle a little over a mile up the river and you will see the waterfront and a marina at Anahuac. Continue northwest a little over two miles, past Lake Anahuac and a number of fishing shacks to Jack's Pass. There are a couple of channels around some trees here. Follow the channel around and paddle south and then southwest out of the pass into Trinity Bay. You are likely to see several alligators on this route and many birds as well.

After entering Trinity Bay, paddle southeast a little less than three miles in open water. Look for the oil and gas platform as a landmark at about 2.5 miles from the headland at Jack's Pass. From here you will see the opening into the Trinity River channel. Turn north along the Trinity River for more than a mile before you turn right into the channel past the bird observation deck to return to the boat ramp at Fort Anahuac. We initially did this route in the opposite direction to take advantage of the river current but discovered that finding Jack's Pass from Trinity Bay was difficult, and we became lost in the adjacent waterway. If you have done the route before, or are familiar with the area, it is smarter to do the route in reverse and take advantage of the river current. This is a beautiful route but requires a GPS unit and a good map of the area to be safe. Camping is available with restrooms and showers and there are also many other places to launch in the park (see earlier Accommodations section for details on camping).

Paddlers are likely to see several American alligators (*Alligator mississippiensis*) along this route. These animals can get quite large, males in excess of 14 feet and females just under 10 feet. Although alligators are capable of killing people, they generally do not attack unless provoked. Stay clear of the animals in the spring and early summer. You will hear the males bellowing to attract females in the spring. Females lay 20–50 goose-sized eggs and cover them with vegetation and mud along the shoreline. The decomposing plant material generates heat and incubates the eggs. Warmer temperatures between 90 and 93 degrees Fahrenheit result in males; while temperatures between 82 and 86 degrees Fahrenheit result in only females. After a 65-day incubation period, the newly hatched young stay

Fort Anahuac/Trinity River Delta Loop

INTERMEDIATE TO ADVANCED

9.3 miles

Drive down the bluff at the back of Fort Anahuac Park to reach the boat ramp and parking area. There is a boardwalk to the left of the boat ramp that goes over a bridge to an observation deck for viewing birds along the Trinity River. Paddle due west across a channel to with the mother for about five months. Alligators have the strongest bite of any animal. University of Florida researchers measured 2,125 pounds of biting force in a 12-foot individual in captivity. Worse yet are infections associated with alligator bites. Be aware that females are protective of their young and keep a respectful distance!

Turtle Bayou to Lake Anahuac

BEGINNING TO INTERMEDIATE

4.2 miles roundtrip

Launch from White Memorial Park and paddle south-west on Turtle Bayou for about 1.8 miles. At this point you will see the broad expanse of Lake Anahuac. According to the Houston Canoe Club description, when water levels are low there is a nice sand beach under the cypress trees on the left side before enter-ing the lake. Strong winds out of the south may make conditions rough here. As you paddle farther along the shore, you will see a white shell beach. Although there is no shade, this is a nice place to rest and eat lunch. The beach consists almost entirely of shells of the marsh clam (*Rangia cuneata*). This clam was a staple for the local Indians and remains an important food source for wildlife. If you want to add a few miles, consider paddling some distance up White Bayou. This small bayou enters the south side of Turtle Bayou at the launch site. Its narrow waterway is shaded with large trees and is beautiful.

Lake Charlotte Loop

INTERMEDIATE TO ADVANCED

7 miles loop, 5.3 miles Charlotte shoreline

This route must be approached with **extreme caution** and with a good map, GPS, and plenty of time. If you do not have these things, then launch at Cedar Hill Park and paddle the perimeter of the lake, a route of about 5.3 miles, depending on how much you explore the edges of the bald cypress swamp. If you want a challenge and have some time, launch from Cedar Hill Park and paddle south. As you paddle south, you will see a large radio tower that makes a good point of reference. Along the shoreline to your left you will see a fishing pier associated with the park. As you reach

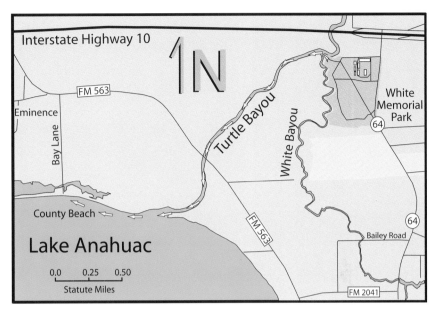

White Memorial Park on Turtle Bayou to County Beach on Lake Anahuac.

Beautiful cypress forests line the perimeter of Lake Charlotte.

the southern shoreline, you may see what appears to be a small weather station along the tree line. Look on your GPS for Mud Lake (see map) and paddle into the cypress swamp toward it from Lake Charlotte. Pick your way through the trees until they open out at Mud Lake. This is the most difficult part. Once you reach

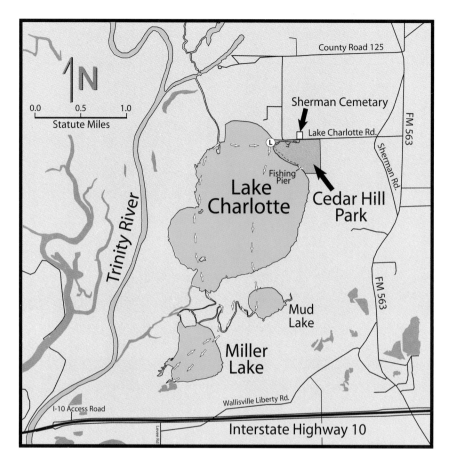

Cedar Hill Park provides access to Lake Charlotte, Mud Lake, and Miller Lake. The extensive cypress swamp forms the northern border of the Trinity River delta. The arrows denote the easiest pathway through Mud Lake to Miller Lake. A GPS receiver is essential if you leave Lake Charlotte.

Indian village and a trading post established by French trader Joseph Blancpain. Look for the waterways at the north end of Miller Lake or paddle back across the lake to your point of entry and proceed back through the trees to the waterway that connects to Mud Lake. When you reach the waterway, paddle northwest for 0.2–0.3 mile. Do not turn south again and follow the waterway, but continue northwest until you reach another waterway that leads you back into Lake Charlotte. Paddle north past a small island to a point on the west side of the lake. The trees at the point are really beautiful and we saw some interesting birds here. Follow the shoreline north and you will see grass at the mouth of the tributary that flows into the lake. This is a pretty waterway that joins with the Trinity River. If you decide to paddle this, it adds on another 1.4 miles to the trip. Depending on tides and recent rainfall, the current into the lake can be strong.

West Galveston Bay Complex

This section of coastline encompasses three selected kayak routes: (1) around Galveston and Pelican islands; (2) from Christmas Bay into San Luis Pass, West Bay, and Chocolate Bayou; and (3) Armand Bayou off Clear Lake, a secondary embayment off West Galveston Bay. Follet's Island and Galveston Island are typical barrier islands, but the sandy dunes are smaller than along other parts of the coast, and human disturbance and development have had major impacts. In fact, it is the history and development of Galveston that makes the area worth visiting. Beaches separated by rocky groins along the Galveston seawall provide experienced paddlers a good place to test their surf skills. Circumnavigating Pelican Island, paddlers can see the hustle and bustle of the Port of Galveston with its cargo docks and large cruise ship terminal. Adjacent to the port facilities along the southeastern part of Pelican Island is Seawolf Park with the 1940s destroyer *USS Stewart* and the old Gato-class submarine *USS Cavalla*.

At the less developed west end of Galveston Island is San Luis Pass. While dangerous for novice and intermediate paddlers, the breakers off San Luis Pass can serve as a playground for the experienced. The

Mud Lake, paddle across it to the southwestern shore, where the outflow is. Follow the waterway for a short distance southwest, then the meander northwest for less than a quarter of a mile. Then follow the bend to paddle southwest again for 0.3–0.4 mile. The waterway will turn north again, but do not follow.

Instead, continue southwest through the trees and pick your way less than 0.2 mile into Miller Lake. Continue southeast across the lake and you will discover among the trees a large berm where you can land. South of the berm is an outflow or another small lake completely covered with dense free-floating mats of water hyacinth (*Eichhornia crassipes*). This nonnative aquatic plant is thought to come from the Amazon River basin and was first introduced to New Orleans in 1884; it is a pest, difficult to control for a variety of reasons, including seeds that are viable for twenty years. The berm is thought to be near the site of both an old marshes, beaches, and sand bars that line the bays and bayous of the East Bay complex are interesting places to fish and observe wildlife. Much effort has gone into revitalizing these important ecosystems as described earlier.

For a small island approximately 27 miles long and less than 3 miles wide, Galveston Island is steeped in Texas history. Its lore includes tales of Indians, explorers, and pirates. It has been known for immigration, seaborne commerce, and much more. It was also the site of the greatest natural disaster in American history. Although it remains an important port today, its primary source of revenue is now from tourism. To understand Galveston, we have to understand its history.

Mexico designated Galveston as a port of entry in 1825. During the Texas Revolution the port was occupied by the Texas Navy. After the war Michael Menard and a group of investors bought land for development and began selling Galveston lots in 1838. The port grew primarily from cotton exports, farming imports, and immigration. Since no banks were chartered at the time, mercantile firms along the Strand handled all the financial transactions and came to be known as the "Wall Street of the Southwest." This has now become a thirty-six-block historic district with art galleries, souvenirs, antiques, and excellent restaurants. Although the Civil War devastated Galveston business, the city was quick to recover. In fact, the busy little port became the state's largest city by 1870 and remained so in 1880. The federal government deepened the natural shipping channel and built the first protective jetty system in 1889. A wagon bridge to the island was completed in 1893. In 1891 the University of Texas Medical Branch (UTMB) became the first medical school in the state.

The Great Storm of 1900 remains the worst natural disaster in the history of the United States. That hurricane killed more than six thousand Galveston residents, and some say nearly as many died on the mainland. After the previous hurricane in 1886 a seawall had been suggested, but no action had been taken. After the 1900 hurricane it was noted that buildings behind large piles of rubble about six blocks from the beach had been spared and that a seawall could

work. The plan included both the seawall and raising the grade or elevation of the island behind it. The initial project began in 1902 with completion of the last extension in 1961. The Galveston seawall and raised grade have proven effective time after time as the city weathered hurricanes in 1909, 1915, 1919, 1932, 1941, 1943, 1949, 1957, Carla in 1961, Alicia in 1983, and most recently Ike in 2008. At 15 to 16 feet above sea level, 30 feet wide, and 10.4 miles long, the seawall has be-

The dense forests around Lake Charlotte are teeming with wildlife.

*Early morning light on
Lake Charlotte.*

come one of the world's longest protective structures. Kayakers can launch from the beaches between short stone jetties that help prevent erosion along the sea-wall and can paddle along the Galveston waterfront.

In the 1920s, the port began to decline as shipping shifted to Houston. Although many factors were at work, this decline was also related to the city's lack of space and adequate water supplies available for industry. During the 1920s and 1930s gambling, illegal drinking, and prostitution made Galveston the "sin city" of the Gulf. The citizens tolerated these activities until 1957, when Attorney General Will Wilson with the cooperation of Texas Rangers shut down drinking establishments, destroyed gambling equipment, and closed many brothels. Gambling returned with the cruise ship trade in the 1990s.

Texas A&M University established the Department

of Oceanography in 1949 and began research vessel operations out of Galveston in 1950. Since then, Texas A&M has grown to include the Texas Maritime Academy at the Fort Crocket Campus on Galveston Island and the Mitchell Campus at Pelican Island along the Galveston Ship Channel. As you paddle past the Pelican Island campus you will probably see the 524-foot training ship *Sirius*.

In the early 1960s the City of Galveston financed a major port restoration project that eventually paid off. The highest tonnage exported from the port was recorded in 1984. In 1990 the Galveston Cruise Ship Terminal was dedicated and began operation. The terminal underwent a $10.6 million renovation in 2000 to accommodate Carnival Cruise Lines, the largest cruise line in the world. Among other sights along the Galveston Ship Channel, you will also see the 205-foot steel-hulled sailing ship *Elissa* moored near the Texas Seaport Museum.

Like many places, the more you know about this area, the more intriguing it becomes. Paddlers can experience oyster reefs along quiet marshes and bay-side beaches with excellent fishing and birdwatching opportunities. Paddlers can also surf the outer coast along the historic Galveston waterfront or watch cargo and cruise ships along the ship channel.

Recommended Navigational Aids
Boater's Map of Galveston Bay Area (With GPS) and *Wade Fishing Map of West Galveston Bay Area (With GPS)* by Hook-N-Line Map Company; *Christmas Bay Paddling Photomap, Armand Bayou Paddling Trail Photomap* and *Galveston Island State Park Paddling Trail* by Shoreline Publishing; aerial maps downloaded from Texas Parks and Wildlife (www.tpwd.state.tx.us/fish-boat/boat/paddlingtrails/coastal/), TerraServer (www.terraserver.com), Google Earth (http://earth.google.com), or MapQuest (www.mapquest.com).

Planning Considerations
Avoid paddling behind San Luis Pass in West Bay and in the vicinity of Christmas Point Reef during very low tides. In the vicinity of Bird Island behind San Luis Pass is a series of shallow sand bars that can be confusing and frustrating to paddlers at low tide. In the Christmas Reef area, what often looks like open water is a complex of shallow jagged oyster reefs. A GPS unit with photomap is useful in this area. Paddlers should not rely solely on photomaps without GPS, as some markers are incorrectly placed on photomaps, and some of the markers are damaged or missing.

Avoid paddling in the Galveston Ship Channel on busier weekends and holidays as the increased boat traffic poses a hazard. When paddling the ship channel, stay clear of all boat traffic and avoid paddling in the middle of the channel. Depending on the wind, the water along the east side of the ship channel and Bolivar Roads around Seawolf Park can be rough. Those who choose to circumnavigate Pelican Island should always check conditions before embarking. Also avoid launching and landing from Galveston beaches where

The steel-hulled schooner Elissa *originally visited the port of Galveston back in the late 1800s. Today a volunteer crew still sails and maintains the ship as part of a bygone era.*

One of the larger grain elevators along the Gulf of Mexico loads grain into cargo ships from all over the world.

many surfers are present. Be careful at San Luis Pass when driving on the beach, as many unwary motorists get stuck in the sand.

For most emergencies, a VHF radio or a cell phone is adequate. If calling from your cell phone, the Galveston Coast Guard Station number is 409-766-5633. For emergencies dial 911 or call the Brazoria County sheriff at 979-849-2441 and in Galveston County call 409-766-2322.

Accommodations

Paddlers interested in visiting San Luis Pass or Christmas Bay can camp for free on the beach by the bridge on the southwest side of San Luis Pass. Just west of the bridge, San Luis County Park has nice air-conditioned cabins to rent for three to twelve people, RV sites, and a boat ramp (979-233-6026, www.brazoriacountyparks.com/San_Luis_Pass/index.asp). Paddlers frequently stay at Galveston Island State Park, 10 miles west of 61st Street in Galveston (www.tpwd.state.tx.us/spdest/findadest/parks/galveston/; reservations 512-389-8900 or www.tpwd.state.tx.us). Facilities at the park have long included screened shelters, campsites with water and electricity, restrooms with showers, and outdoor showers convenient for washing off gear. Some facilities have not been replaced since Hurricane Ike in 2008; check with the park for details. Galveston offers accommodations too numerous to list (www.galveston.com/lodging/). For those interested in paddling Armand Bayou, there are many options because of its proximity to the Johnson Space Center and the University of Houston Clear Lake campus (www.spacecenter.org/VisitorServicesHotels.html). For those interested in paddling Chocolate Bayou, Camp Mohawk County Park is an option (281-581-2319, www.brazoriacountyparks.com/Mohawk/index.asp).

Directions to Launch Sites
Galveston: From Houston, travel south on Interstate 45 across the causeway and take 61st Street south to the seawall. Turn left on Seawall Boulevard and look for parking along the seawall. Alternatively, drive east along Seawall Boulevard to Stewart Beach at 6th Street, which has restrooms and showers. Another

choice is East Beach, also called Apffel Park. To get to East Beach, continue along Seawall Boulevard and turn right on Apffel Road. The road terminates on the beach at the park. The big difference between the two beaches is that no alcohol consumption is allowed at Stewart Beach, which is generally considered a family-oriented park.

Galveston Ship Channel: From Houston, drive south on Interstate 45 over the causeway to Galveston Island, where I-45 turns into Avenue J. Turn left on 25th Street for about 9 blocks and then turn right on Avenue A. Follow Avenue A past the UTMB Hospital and turn left on 4th Street or North Holiday Drive. The Galveston Yacht Club is on your left (409-762-9689 ext. 201, www.galvestonyachtclub.com). Kayakers can launch from the club's boat ramp into the Galveston Ship Channel for $10/boat. To access the channel from Pelican Island, turn left on 51st Street in Galveston and cross the causeway to Pelican Island, where you are on Seawolf Parkway. There are two launch options. If you can obtain permission from the Police Department at Texas A&M Galveston in advance (Mitchell Campus, 409-740-4545, www.tamug.edu), you can launch from the boat ramp in the small boat basin. A more difficult launch is at the end of Seawolf Parkway in Seawolf Park, where paddlers sometimes obtain permission to launch from the rocks on the protected west side of the park adjacent to the parking lot.

Galveston Island State Park: From 61st Street in Galveston, turn right or west on Seawall Boulevard and drive 10 miles to the main park entrance and turn left to pay the park entry fee at the toll booth. Enter the park here to access camping and to paddle on the Gulf of Mexico side of the island (see map). To access the bay paddling trails where there is calmer water, drive back past the toll booth and continue across FM 3005 northwest toward the bay on Park Road 66. Take the first left southwest on Clapper Rail Road (may be unmarked) to reach the launch area for the Jenkins Bayou Trail at the end of the road. If you continue a short distance past Clapper Rail Road on Park Road 66, you will see the launch area for the Oak Bayou Trail on your left. At the end of Park Road 66 is the put-in for the Dana Cove Trail. Just east of the parking area is a short trail that ends on a small sandy beach suitable for launching on Lake Como.

San Luis Pass: Take Highway 288 south from Houston and turn left on FM 523. Drive 19.5 miles on FM 523 and turn left onto the Bluewater Highway/CR 257 at Surfside. Drive 13.1 miles to San Luis Pass. Just before the bridge you will see a bait shop and gas station on your left. Turn left here onto China Clipper Drive. As you turn, take an immediate right down a rough service road that parallels the Bluewater Highway. Drive toward the pass about 0.1 mile. From here you can either turn left to enter San Luis County Park, and use their boat ramp to launch, or continue straight ahead to launch from the beach along San Luis Pass. Approximately 2.4 miles before San Luis Pass you can turn left at the sign for Ernie's Too bait camp and drive less than a third of a mile up Amigo Lane to use a public boat ramp to launch into Christmas Bay and Churchill Bayou.

Chocolate Bayou: From Houston, drive south on Highway 288 and turn left or southeast on Highway 6 toward Alvin. Drive 11.2 miles and turn right on the South Alvin Bypass to merge onto Highway 35 south. After approximately 7.5 miles you will cross Chocolate Bayou. Just after the bridge there is a small park on the left. Currently there is no signage, but this is Chocolate Bayou County Park. Pull in and drive down to the parking area adjacent to the boat ramp on the bayou. To launch at Albert Finkle Memorial County Park at Liverpool, continue about 0.5 mile south of the Chocolate Bayou bridge on Highway 35 and turn left on CR 192 to Liverpool. In Liverpool turn left again on CR 171 or Calhoun Street. As you drive northeast you will notice the road forks just before crossing another bridge across Chocolate Bayou. Stay left on Calhoun Street and you will see Albert Finkle Memorial County Park on your right just below the CR 171 bridge over the bayou. Drive south through Liverpool on Main Street to get to Amsterdam. This turns into CR 203 and comes close to the water in the small community of Amsterdam. Turn left on CR 203A or Johanson Drive and launch at Peterson Landing, the boat ramp next to the old restaurant and bait shop.

Armand Bayou: Take Interstate 45 south from Houston and turn east on NASA Road 1. Just past the Johnson Space Center you will cross the bridge where Armand Bayou enters Clear Lake. On the left side is Clear Lake Park, where you can launch off the grassy shoreline or the paddling club docks. On the right is a small parking area with a boat ramp where you can launch on Clear Lake and paddle under the bridge into Mud Lake and up Armand Bayou. Alternatively, drive southeast from Houston's Beltway 8 on Red Bluff Road and turn right on Bay Area Boulevard. You will pass Armand Bayou Nature Center on the left. Continue a little more than half a mile to Bay Area Park on the left. Follow the entrance road to a small parking area along the bayou where you can launch.

The Galveston Waterfront

INTERMEDIATE TO ADVANCED, WITH SURF EXPERIENCE
variable distances

There are three options here. First, you can park on the seawall and launch from one of the beaches along it. Great care must be taken to avoid rock breakwaters, and surfers may also present a hazard. However, the breakwaters provide a great place to take pictures of kayakers surfing. You can also launch and land either at Stewart Beach or East Beach (Apffel Park). Stewart Beach is the better option.

Side Trips

In Galveston, Moody Gardens offers an aquarium, botanical garden, and natural history museum well worth visiting (800-582-4673, www.moodygardens.com). Several other museums are worth a visit: Galveston Railroad Museum (409-765-5700, www.galvestonrrmuseum.com), Lone Star Flight Museum (888-359-5736, www.lsfm.org), Oceanstar Offshore Drilling Rig and Museum (409-766-STAR, www.oceanstaroec.com), and the Texas Seaport Museum (409-763-1877, www.galvestonhistory.org/Texas_Seaport_Museum.asp). On Pelican Island, Seawolf Park is also worth a visit (409–797–5114, www.galveston.com/seawolfpark/).

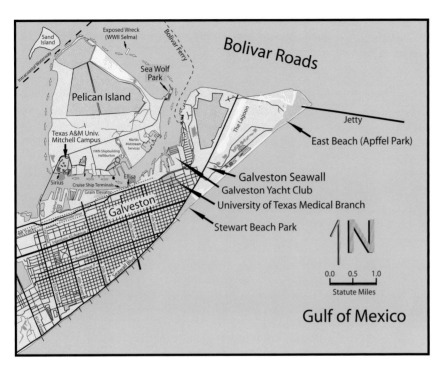

The city of Galveston and Pelican Island. The arrows denote the circumnavigation of Pelican Island from the Galveston Yacht Club.

Galveston Island Ship Channel and Pelican Island Circumnavigation

INTERMEDIATE TO ADVANCED

7.8 miles

This route passes part of the Bolivar Roads channel, Texas City channel, and intracoastal waterway and goes through the busy port of Galveston, where paddlers can see historic ships and seaborne commerce. I have launched with permission from the staff at Seawolf Park and on the north side of Pelican Island, and I understand visitors may be able to get permission to launch from Texas A&M Mitchell Campus on Pelican Island (see Directions to Launch Sites). Launching for a fee from the Galveston Yacht Club near the Bolivar ferry terminal is the safest, best option. The east end of the Galveston Ship Channel and the northeast side of Pelican Island can be rough. In addition to getting local weather reports, it is wise to check the water conditions and wind from Seawolf Park before deciding to circumnavigate the island.

Launch from the boat ramp at the Galveston Yacht Club and paddle southwest along the cargo docks, where you will see the large cranes for load-ing and unloading ships. Farther down the channel is the Ocean Star Offshore Drilling Rig and museum. When I last paddled the channel, you could look at the retired Ocean Star rig and then glance across the channel to where two modern oil platforms were being constructed. The 1877 steel-hulled tall ship *Elissa* is moored just beyond this museum and is part of the Texas Seaport Museum. Built in Scotland, the *Elissa* serviced many ports, including Galveston, during her time as a merchant ship. She was rediscovered in Greece and brought back to the United States to be restored in Galveston. Her nineteen sails constitute 11,500 feet of cloth controlled by miles of rigging and a volunteer crew. On one trip I was able to paddle up to the *Elissa* and talk to the volunteers working on her rigging. As I turned to continue up the channel, I could not help but notice the juxtaposition between my primitive kayak, the old steel-hulled schooner, and the Carnival cruise liner just ahead. There were men working along her waterline on a small platform, mak-ing repairs and painting. Once I passed the cruise ship terminals, a monolithic grain elevator came into view, with grain being loaded into freighters from Bangkok and Korea. Thousands of birds were congregating all over the facility. This is a good place to cross the chan-nel to get a look at the Texas A&M Mitchell Campus, where the training ship *Sirius* is usually moored.

Paddle under the Pelican Island causeway and turn north along the island shoreline. Paddle 2 miles north and turn northeast through a small pass that separates Pelican Island from Sand Island. Watch for barge traffic, as this is part of the Gulf Intracoastal Waterway. There are often numerous barges parked along the sandy shores here. Continue around the island southeast along the sandy shoreline past a large shallow lagoon. You can land on the beach and look over a sandy berm into the lagoon to watch birds. Also watch for fossils emerging from the eroding mudstone scattered along the shoreline. A friend of mine reported finding some mammoth bones here a number of years ago. Continue southeast along the shore and you will see the exposed wreck of the Selma, a concrete cargo ship from WWII. There are ragged holes in the hull where steel rebar is exposed in places, showing the old ship's construction.

Paddle southeast again toward the fishing pier at Seawolf Park. The park is home to the decommissioned 1940s destroyer *USS Stewart* and the old Gato-class submarine *USS Cavalla*. The park was built on an old immigration station site as a memorial for the famed WWII submarine *USS Seawolf.* The famous submarine damaged or sank forty enemy ships during her first fourteen patrols. Her crew of eighty-three and seventeen passengers were lost near Australia under mysterious circumstances sometime after October 3, 1944. Like the *Seawolf,* the *USS Cavalla* was also a decorated WWII Gato-class submarine. It was famous for the action during its maiden voyage, when it sank the 30,000-ton Japanese aircraft carrier *Shokaku,* a veteran of fighting in the Coral Sea and Pearl Harbor. The 307-foot *USS Stewart,* a WWII destroyer escort, is adjacent to the submarine. It was primarily a training ship and was decommissioned in late 1945. If you wish to land to look around, you can land to the right of the pier along the shoreline. Be careful if you land on the rocks. If you continue left around the pier, stay clear of the fisherman there and along the rocks. Paddle around the Seawolf Park pavilion and turn south back into the Galveston Ship Channel past the *USS Cavalla* and *USS Stewart.* Do not cross the channel to arrive back at the Galveston Yacht Club boat ramp until after you pass the ferry terminal.

Galveston Island State Park

BEGINNING TO INTERMEDIATE

2.6, 2.8, and 4.8 miles

Three trails have been established for kayakers: Dana Cove (2.6 miles), Oak Bayou (4.8 miles), and Jenkins Bayou (2.8 miles). They are located along the bay side of the state park and showcase some of the work being done to restore Galveston Bay's marshland and sea grass beds. The Texas Parks and Wildlife Department maintains a website with information on these and other coastal paddling trails (www.tpwd.state.tx.us/fishboat/boat/paddlingtrails/coastal/). The mileages given are those officially listed on the TPWD maps and website descriptions.

Dana Cove Trail: From the launch site on Lake Como at the end of the park road, paddle north

▲ *Care must be taken to avoid barge traffic in the intracoastal waterway between Sand and Pelican islands.*

◄ *The remnants of the cargo ship Selma are a well-known landmark off Pelican Island.*

through the shallows and across Dana Cove. Paddle southeast through a gap in the breakwater made of sand-filled geotextile tubes and back to the launch site. Behind the breakwater sea grasses have recolonized extensively. You can follow GPS markers #1–8 if you

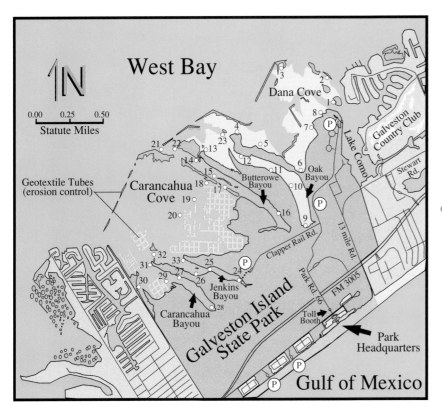

Galveston Island State Park. P denotes parking areas adjacent to launch sites. Numbered GPS markers on the bay side of the park mark the Dana Cove, Oak Bayou, and Jenkins Bayou paddling trails established and maintained by Texas Parks and Wildlife.

want the official route, but it is generally more fun to paddle where you wish and use the markers as a reference for your location.

Oak Bayou Trail: Paddle north and then northwest along Oak Bayou less than one mile to marker #13. Paddle southwest through a short channel to marker #14 and turn southeast along Butterowe Bayou. You can paddle all the way down past marker #16 or turn west at marker #17 on the west side of the bayou to enter Carancahua Cove. Here you will see more geotextile tubes used to form restoration terraces where cordgrass has been planted. Paddle southwest along the terraces and then loop north to markers #21 and #22. Paddle east to marker #23 and then turn south into Oak Bayou to get back to the parking area.

Jenkins Bayou Trail: The GPS markers for this route do not follow in sequence. I suggest you just use these markers as a general reference for location. Launch from the small beach at the end of Clapper Rail Road and paddle northwest along Jenkins Bayou. You

will see markers #24, #25, and #26, then #33 and #32. Paddle southwest from marker #32 along some terraces and southeast into Carancahua Bayou before looping back northwest. Paddle east from marker #31 and then southeast along Jenkins Bayou back to your launch site. Interestingly, there is a circular pond north of the parking lot. This is all that remains of a large development that was to include residences, a zoo, hotel, railroad, and racetrack. The effort was abandoned after the hurricane in 1900.

San Luis Pass
INTERMEDIATE TO ADVANCED
variable mileage

We often camp on and launch from the sandy beach near the bridge on the southwest side of San Luis Pass, but many paddlers also launch from the boat ramp at San Luis Pass County Park. Be careful if you launch from the sandy beach adjacent to the pass, as many unwary visitors get vehicles stuck in the sand here. If you paddle from the bridge instead of the boat ramp at the county park to access West Bay or Cold Pass, then add 0.6 mile to your roundtrip.

Open Gulf/Surfing: Paddlers can access the open Gulf and surf if experience and training permit. DANGER: avoid paddling here during adverse weather or when strong tidal currents are present or can be predicted.

Bird Island
INTERMEDIATE
2.8 miles roundtrip to Bird Island, 3.6 miles roundtrip to the bar north of Bird Island

Paddle from San Luis County Park directly across Cold Pass to the Mud Island shoreline (marker #16). Paddle north into the channel along the east side of Bird Island. Many people fish off the exposed sand bar along the east side of this channel. An extensive bar extends to the north of Bird Island. There is a good landing spot on the north side of the bar, but it should be used only if there are no birds present. If you have GPS, this can be a route to get to Chocolate Bayou for experienced paddlers with open water experience. The shallow channels and sand bars can be difficult to navigate across if the tide is low. Paddlers attempting to paddle from the bridge at San Luis Pass directly to Bird Island have difficulty paddling across the shallow bars, and it may be impossible to cross these bars at low tide.

Mud Island Circumnavigation

ADVANCED

7.9–8.5 miles

Starting at San Luis Pass County Park, paddle across Cold Pass to Mud Island and follow the shoreline north less than 2 miles. You will see several fishing shacks that mark the entrance to the channel that skirts the northwest side of Mud Island. Paddle past the inlet to the beaches just beyond. This is a great place to rest and birdwatch in the marshes behind the shell beaches, which extend for more than a mile past the inlet. Those interested can paddle along these beaches

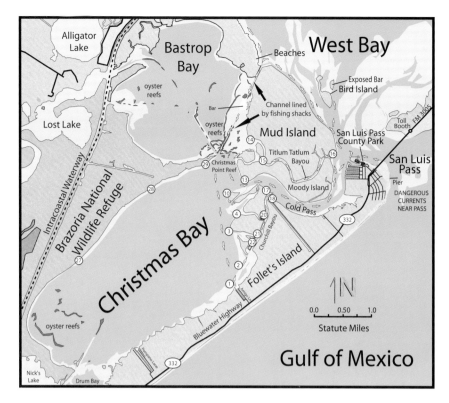

▲ The San Luis Pass area and Christmas Bay. Numbered GPS markers have been placed to guide paddlers through this area. The arrows mark some of the routes around and through Mud Island

◀ Fishing shacks and extensive oyster reefs line the channel along the north side of Mud Island.

to extend their trip. Paddle back south and turn southwest into the channel lined by fishing shacks and oyster reef. A little over half a mile down the channel, you will encounter a narrow channel through oyster reef with a shallow bar beyond. If you look far beyond, you will see more fishing shacks lining the channel. To get to them, you must turn southeast toward the Mud Island shoreline to find the shallow channel around the bar. If the tide is too low, this becomes an impasse and paddlers have to abort the route and return the way they came. Once around the bar, head toward the shacks lining the submerged channel to get back on course. Continue until you reach a point of land on your right. This is Christmas Point and you will be surrounded by Christmas Point Reef. Paddle due east from here along the face of a barrier oyster reef toward the shoreline. Then turn south and follow the shoreline into Cold Pass back to San Luis County Park. Alternatively, to shorten your paddle, you can follow the shoreline left (northeast) and into a small inlet that becomes Titlum Tatlum Bayou.

Moody Island Circumnavigation

INTERMEDIATE

6.0 miles

Starting at San Luis Pass County Park, paddle west across Cold Pass into Titlum Tatlum Bayou. As you turn southwest you will paddle past many fishing shacks lining the bayou. After more than half a mile you will turn northwest and then meander through the bayou past marker #15. Ahead the bayou forks and you can paddle either way around the Moody Island shoreline south to Cold Pass to return to San Luis Pass County Park.

Christmas Bay/Churchill Bayou

INTERMEDIATE

4.3 miles

Launch from the public boat ramp at the end of Amigo Lane and paddle north into Christmas Bay. To your right, you will see extensive marshland with several channels and inlets. Continue north past marker #10 and turn east into Cold Pass for approximately two-thirds of a mile. At marker #17, turn south into Churchill Bayou. As you return to the starting point,

stay right or away from the Follet's Island shoreline to avoid very shallow water with jagged patches of oysters.

Lower Chocolate Bayou

BEGINNING TO INTERMEDIATE

8.5 miles one way, 17 miles roundtrip

Launch at Peterson Landing in Amsterdam. On our first trip, Ken Johnson and I were delayed until 3:30 P.M. by thunderstorms and paddled north to arrive at Albert Finkle County Park at Liverpool by dusk. We paddled back down the bayou at night and in the rain. It was a great trip, but we were exhausted. After we dined at their restaurant adjacent to Peterson's Landing, the owners allowed us to camp in the grass in their front yard next to some ancient fishing boats instead of driv-

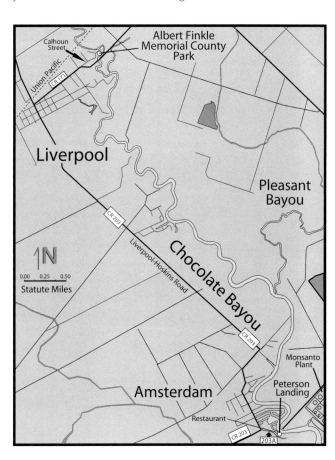

Lower Chocolate Bayou from Peterson Landing in Amsterdam to Albert Finkle Memorial County Park.

ing back to Galveston Island. They were surprised that we could go so far so quickly in our small craft in such cold and rainy weather conditions. This is a fun trip because of the wildlife, some interesting homes, and the wreck of a large shrimp boat in the channel. Finkle County Park is an excellent place to stop for lunch if doing a roundtrip.

Upper Chocolate Bayou

INTERMEDIATE

5.8 miles one way, 11.6 miles roundtrip
Launch on the north end from Chocolate Bayou County Park or farther south from Albert Finkle County Park in Liverpool. At the time I surveyed this route after a January storm, there were trees blocking the waterway about 1.9 miles south of Chocolate Bayou County Park. In addition to this portage, the route requires traversing a coffer dam about 3.6–3.7 miles south of Chocolate Bayou County Park. I observed some very large alligator gar (*Atractosteus spatula*) above the dam. The back of one of these giants was about as wide as a German shepherd. As earlier noted, these fish may live more than 75 years, reach 9 feet long or more, and tip the scales at more than 350 pounds. I observed more wildlife on this route than along the lower bayou. However, the lower section of the bayou is more scenic than the upper section.

Armand Bayou from Clear Lake Park to Red Bluff Road

INTERMEDIATE

6 miles, 12 miles roundtrip (14 miles with addition of Horsepen Bayou)
Although there are GPS markers throughout the bayou that provide accurate locations with a good map, some are missing. GPS maps can be purchased from the Armand Bayou Nature Center or downloaded from the Texas Parks and Wildlife website and are highly recommended. This is one of the most accessible places to observe alligators along the Texas coast. Launch from the grass or from the small docks used by the Bay Area Rowing Club at Clear Lake Park into Mud Lake at the entrance of Armand Bayou. Alternatively, you can launch from the public boat ramp across NASA Road 1

on Clear Lake and paddle north under the bridge into Mud Lake. Less than 1 mile north toward the end of Mud Lake are signs prohibiting motorized watercraft from entering the bayou. At approximately 1.7 miles you will see the entrance to Horsepen Bayou between GPS markers 8 and 9. Horsepen Bayou is one of the most beautiful parts of the reserve, but it can be shallow, depending on the tide. It is approximately 1 mile from the mouth of the bayou to GPS marker #14 if you take the detour, adding two miles.

On my first trip to the reserve I was amazed by the birds and beautiful vegetation with flowers blooming everywhere. I did not see any other people. At approximately 2.8 miles from Clear Lake Park, you reach Bay

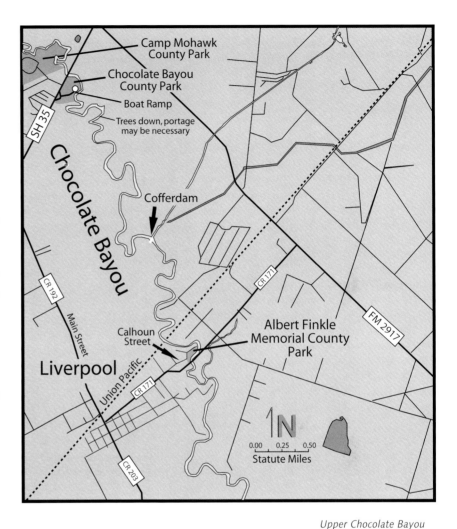

Upper Chocolate Bayou can be challenging as portages around trees and over a cofferdam may be necessary.

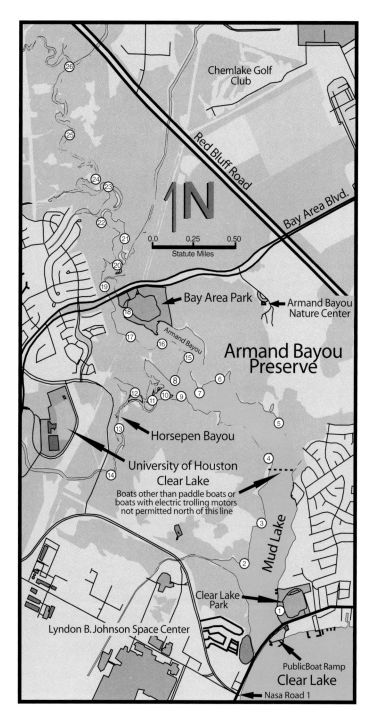

Armand Bayou Nature Center close to the Lyndon B. Johnson Space Center protects one of the last areas where coastal prairie can be seen in Texas. This is also an ideal area to view birds and alligators. Numbered GPS markers are used by paddlers for navigational purposes.

Area Park and the Bay Area Boulevard bridge just beyond. The park makes a nice rest stop and often a place to visit with other paddlers. It is also the most popular place to launch and is close to the Armand Bayou Nature Center (see next route). After paddling under the bridge, stay left to continue up the bayou. You may see marker #19 as you pass through a narrow passage into a small lake. The narrow channel to continue north is to the far right on the southeast corner of the lake. As you paddle north, you will see stands of marsh cordgrass broken down to form alligator nests along the bank. Look for alligators sunning themselves along the shore. Just past marker #26 the channel straightens along a row of pine trees and the waterway ends at the Red Bluff Road bridge. Retrace your route back down the bayou to get back to Clear Lake Park.

Upper Armand Bayou from Bay Area Park to Cedar Bluff Road

BEGINNER TO INTERMEDIATE

6.4 miles roundtrip

Launch from Bay Area Park and paddle north under the Bay Area Boulevard bridge. Stay left along the shoreline to find the channel going up the bayou. You may see marker #19 as you proceed through the channel into a small lake. This lake is beautiful and worth exploring, and the outlet to go on up the bayou is on the southeast part of the lake. Continue up the bayou and you will likely see many alligators. Although these animals are unlikely to be aggressive, keep a respectful distance so as not to disturb or antagonize them.

Horsepen Bayou

BEGINNING TO INTERMEDIATE

4 miles roundtrip

Launch from Bay Area Park into Armand Bayou and paddle south around the park. As you round the next bend, paddle southwest along the right side of the bayou. You will pass a small headland at marker #8 and see a lake to the northwest, but continue southwest into Horsepen Bayou. This area may be difficult to navigate when tides are low because of shallow water. However, this is a very beautiful bayou and a great place to take pictures. ∎

Armand Bayou serves as an excellent example of a riparian hardwood forest and coastal prairie that hosts a variety of wildlife.

Bryan Beach State Park to Matagorda Bay Nature Park

THE COLORADO, SAN BERNARD, AND Brazos river outflows cause wide fluctuations in salinity, sedimentation, and changes in coastal morphology. These conditions favor more extensive oyster beds and rich marshlands that attract millions of birds each year. Birdwatching and fishing are excellent for kayakers. However, great care must be taken in some of the shallow bays to avoid becoming stranded on jagged oysters hiding in these turbid waters. Camping is good along the outer coast and along sand spits associated with these rivers.

The Spaniards called it Río de los Brazos de Dios, "River of the Arms of God." Now known as the Brazos River, this waterway extends 1,280 miles from its source in New Mexico to the Gulf of Mexico, making it the eleventh longest in the country, draining nearly 45,000 square miles of territory. The outflow along the coast is an interesting area for paddlers to explore and can be accessed from Bryan Beach State Park. From wave action and storm activity at the mouth of the river, large trees have been embedded along the southwest beach, jutting skyward 10 to 20 feet at random odd angles to give the area a bizarre "devil's playground" appearance. Behind the southwest beach on Wolf Island at

Brown pelicans (Pelecanus occidentalis) *patrol the beach fishing along the southwest side of the Brazos River outflow.*

the mouth of the Brazos River is rich wetland habitat good for birdwatching. The old outflow of the Brazos River was cut off in 1929 to prevent flooding in Freeport Harbor and the Freeport Ship Channel, now one of the state's largest deepwater ports. Although surrounded by industrialization and not recommended for paddling, Quintana Beach County Park offers convenient RV sites, tent camping with restroom and shower facilities, an interpretive center, and two historic homes.

The Colorado River extends 862 miles from northwest Texas and parallels the Brazos River. Early explorers often confused the two. Originally, the port town of Matagorda was on Matagorda Bay and was an important shipping port in the 1800s for rice, cotton, fish, oysters and beef. The town is the third oldest Anglo settlement in Texas, established by Stephen F. Austin with permission from the Mexican government in 1827. A massive logjam eventually extended 46 miles up the river, blocking traffic and trapping sediments. Efforts to clear the logjam were finally successful in 1929. However, by 1936 the sediments formed a massive delta across the bay, separating East Matagorda Bay from the main bay. Later that year a canal that remains today was dredged from Matagorda to the Gulf of Mexico. The road that parallels the canal provides access to East Matagorda Bay for paddlers interested in fishing and birdwatching. The Lower Colorado River Authority has recently completed development of the 1,600-acre Matagorda Bay Nature Park, which includes tent and RV camping, a natural science center with classrooms and exhibits, guided kayak tours along the bay, and access to 22 miles of beach along the outer coast.

Thousands of years ago, Caney Creek was the old outflow for the Colorado River. Now its wild meandering course, typical of old streams, passes through rich agricultural land where rice and cotton are grown and cattle are raised. It flows past the small town of Sargent, across the intracoastal waterway and into the Gulf of Mexico through Mitchell's Cut. Prior to the Civil War sugar and cotton production was so successful that the lower reaches of the Caney Creek outflow were often referred to as "plantation row." Some of the stately homes still exist, and ruins of an old sugar mill and saw mill are still evident. Kayakers have excellent access to the coastal marshes and wetlands for fishing and birding in

and around Matagorda Peninsula State Park. Mitchell's Cut also provides access to the outer coast, although a large shoal at the mouth of the pass often makes surf conditions dangerous. Paddling up Caney Creek, marshes and wetlands give way to woodland flora and fauna typical of the northern Texas coast.

Although not a major drainage like the Colorado or Brazos rivers, the San Bernard River was one of the few that flowed directly into the Gulf of Mexico until a sandbar blocked its mouth during the spring of 2005. The San Bernard River then flowed into the Gulf of Mexico through the intracoastal waterway and primarily through the mouth of the Brazos River. Significant discharge from the San Bernard interfered with barge traffic heading south. In March of 2009, the Army Corps of Engineers dredged and reopened the river mouth, in response to local pressure for this action. The pass has been renamed Edwards Cut after Roy and Jan Edwards, whose petition ultimately led to the reopening of the San Bernard River to the Gulf. It was the rerouting of the Brazos River in 1929 to stabilize Freeport Harbor that ultimately led to the sand bar formation that blocked the mouth of the San Bernard River. The sand bar at the old river mouth is an excellent place for paddlers to camp. Paddling through the San Bernard National Wildlife Refuge is also excellent, and camping is allowed on the outer coast adjacent to its bays. The refuge is a popular place for birdwatchers to gather in the spring and fall. It is also a popular destination for duck hunters. This refuge is part of the Texas Mid-Coast Wildlife Refuge Complex, which hosts more than 100,000 shorebirds during spring migration and has been designated as an internationally significant shorebird site by the Western Hemisphere Shorebird Reserve Network. At the time of writing, one of the oldest, largest oak trees in the country was discovered on land adjacent to the refuge. This land has been acquired, and there are plans to build a trail into the area to provide public access.

Recommended Navigational Aids

Matagorda Bay and *Freeport Area Fishing Map* by Hook-N-Line Map Company; aerial maps downloaded from TerraServer (www.terraserver.com), Google Earth (http://earth.google.com), or MapQuest (www.mapquest.com).

Planning Considerations

To get more information regarding Matagorda Bay Nature Park, see its web-site (www.lcra.org/parks/ developed_parks/matagorda.html). At the time of writing the park offered kayak tours on a 2.5-mile bay route for 6–12 people for $25–50 per person. The park also offers many educational opportunities. For more information on the kayak tours, call the Lower Colorado River Authority (979-245-4631) or McKinney Roughs Nature Park (800-776-5272).

A cell phone is usually adequate for emergencies. Be prepared to call the Port O'Connor Coast Guard Station at 512-983-2617 or the Freeport Coast Guard Station at 979-233-3801 for emergencies, depending on location. Depending on the county, sheriffs' departments may also be an option. Check with the Coast Guard and county law enforcement offices before your trip.

Accommodations

Tent camping is available on Quintana Island at Bryan Beach State Park, but it is undeveloped. Tent camping and RV sites are available on the island at Quintana Beach County Park. There are also a number of beach houses for rent (www.quintana-tx.org/ places-staryeat.htm). Matagorda Island Nature Park has a 70-site RV park, and tent camping is permitted on the adjacent Gulf Coast beach. There are restrooms, outdoor showers, covered picnic shelters, and a group pavilion. For further information see the park website (www.lcra.org/parks/developed_parks/ matagorda.html) or call 979-863-7120. The nearby town of Matagorda offers vacation rentals, RV parks, and a few motels (www.matagordatexas.com/lodging .htm). Fewer but similar accommodations are available at Sargent along Caney Creek (www.sargenttexas.com/ rentals.htm). Beach camping is permitted along the Gulf of Mexico southeast of Sargent at Matagorda Peninsula State Park. However, the beach park is completely undeveloped, without signage or facilities of any kind.

Directions to Launch Sites

Brazos River Outflow/Bryan Beach State Park: From Houston drive south on Highway 288 to Freeport.

Turn left and drive east on Highway 36 to FM 1495. Turn right and drive south on FM 1495 across the Gulf Intracoastal Waterway to the beach. Turn right to get to the beach area at the mouth of the Brazos River. To get to the mouth of Freeport Harbor and Quintana Beach County Park, take FM 1495 across the intracoastal waterway and turn left on Quintana Street or FM 723. Turn right on 5th Street to reach the county park and turn right on 8th Street to gain beach access.

San Bernard National Wildlife Refuge: From Houston go south on Highway 288 to FM 2004. Drive southwest on FM 2004 across Highway 36, where the road turns into FM 2611, to reach FM 2918. Turn left to go south on FM 2918, which ends at a parking area and boat ramp along the intracoastal waterway adjacent to the wildlife refuge. To access the boat ramp along Cedar Lake Creek within the San Bernard National Wildlife Refuge, follow FM 2918 to CR 306. Turn right on CR 306 and turn left at the park entrance. Follow the park road south to the parking area and boat ramp at the end of the road. To reach this area from Victoria or Corpus Christi, travel to Bay City on Highway 35 and turn southeast on FM 457 to reach FM 2611. Drive northeast on FM 2611, turn right on CR 306, and proceed until you see the entrance of the San Bernard NWR on your right. If you wish to reach the boat ramp on the intracoastal waterway, continue driving until you reach FM 2918. Drive south on FM 2918 until you reach the parking area and boat ramp. Cedar Cut adjacent to the San Bernard NWR can also be accessed by driving approximately 6.4 miles northeast along the Gulf Coast beach from FM 457 south of Sargent.

Sargent Beach and Matagorda Peninsula State Park: To get to Sargent from Houston, go south on Highway 288 to FM 2004. Drive southwest on FM 2004 across Highway 36, where the road turns into FM 2611, to reach FM 457. Turn left and drive south to reach Sargent. From Victoria or Corpus Christi, travel to Bay City on Highway 35 and turn southeast on FM 457 to get to Sargent. To reach the undeveloped Matagorda Peninsula State Park or Mitchell's Cut, continue south on FM 457 until the road ends on Sargent Beach. You can drive on and launch from the beach or turn right at the end of FM 457 and drive west-southwest on Canal Street to reach the West Mooring boat ramp on the intracoastal waterway.

Matagorda Bay Nature Park: From Houston take Highway 288 south to Highway 35. Turn southwest on Highway 35 to reach Bay City. Turn south on Highway 60 to Matagorda. Turn south on FM 2031 and cross the intracoastal waterway and continue until you reach the park. From Corpus Christi or Victoria, travel to Palacios on Highway 35. Follow Highway 35 north from Palacios, then turn right on FM 521 east to Highway 60, and turn south on Highway 60 to Matagorda. Turn south on FM 2031, cross the intracoastal, and continue until you reach the park.

Paddlers have many options to gain access to East Matagorda Bay, the Colorado River, and the Gulf of Mexico from Matagorda Bay Nature Park and FM 2031 south of Matagorda. As you drive south on FM 2031 past the intracoastal waterway pontoon bridge about 1 mile, there is a nice TPWD boat ramp adjacent to River Bend Restaurant to access the Colorado River. To the south of River Bend Restaurant, paddlers can launch and land at St. Mary's Bayou, Rudacell Slough, and a canal south of Rawling's Landing. At the time of writing, Rudacell Slough was closed. The canal just south of Rawling's Landing is an excellent access point for the wetlands that line the southern shoreline of East Matagorda Bay. You can unload boats and equipment at the canal but must park across the road just south of the canal to avoid being towed.

If you drive to the end of FM 2031 into the Matagorda Bay Nature Park, there is a main parking area that pro-

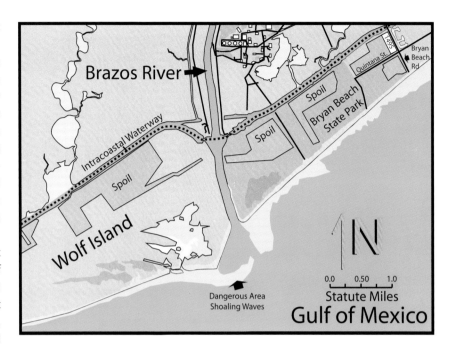

Side Trip

Sea Center Texas is operated by the Texas Parks and Wildlife Department and Coastal Conservation Association as a nature center, aquarium, and fish hatchery. It is located near Freeport at Lake Jackson (979-292-0100, www.tpwd.state.tx.us/spdest/visitorcenters/seacenter/visit/).

vides sheltered beach access at the mouth of the Colorado River (see warnings in the route description). You can also drive down the beach to launch into the Gulf of Mexico. Approximately 2.5 miles down the beach is a washover channel that provides access to Spring Bayou and Three Mile Lake, depending on water levels.

Brazos River Outflow/ Brazos Beach State Park

INTERMEDIATE TO ADVANCED

variable mileage

Launch at the river mouth from Bryan Beach State Park to paddle across the river outflow and southwest behind a sandy shoal with breaking waves along the shore (see map). The beachcombing here is excellent, and severe storm activity has left trees embedded in the sand at strange angles. Some paddlers portage into the shallow bay behind the beach to fish or birdwatch. All paddlers should be cautious, as occasionally strong currents can push paddlers out into an area of strong, breaking waves along the sandy shoal that extends from the southeastern edge of Wolf Island.

▲ *Bryan Beach State Park and the Brazos River outflow. Beware of the shallow bar and shoaling waves at the river mouth.*

San Bernard River Mouth

INTERMEDIATE

5.2 miles

The San Bernard River mouth was opened by the Army Corps of Engineers in March of 2009 and has been named Edwards Cut. The sand beach at the terminus of the Sand Bernard River is a great place to camp. Launch at the boat ramp at the end of FM 2918 and paddle east-northeast to the San Bernard River. Paddle southeast and then south to reach the waterway behind the barrier beach to camp.

Cedar Lakes, Gas Well Cut

INTERMEDIATE

10.8 miles

This route begins from the boat ramp at the end of FM 2918. Paddle approximately 4 miles west-southwest down the intrac-

Unlike along much of the Texas coast, here many trees washed from the Brazos River litter the beaches. Some kayakers paddling in the surf report that submerged trees may represent an unforeseen hazard.

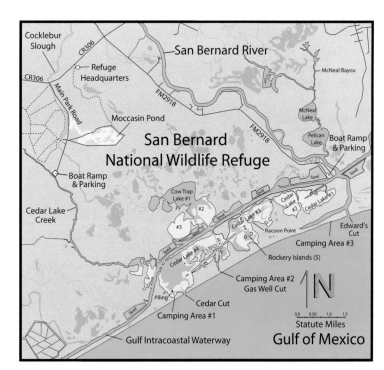

San Bernard National Wildlife Refuge offers outer coast camping accessible from the intracoastal waterway and Cedar Lake Creek.

The beach and dunes adjacent to the San Bernard River outflow are one of the nicest camping areas on the northern coast.

oastal waterway and turn south at the cut leading into the northeastern part of Cedar Lake #4. As you paddle south, you will see a gas platform to the right down a small channel (see map). Continue down the main channel past another gas platform to the end of the channel known as Gas Well Cut to land behind the Gulf beach, where you can make camp. If you portage to paddle the outer coast, beware of the remains of an old pier northeast of the camp site.

San Bernard National Wildlife Refuge Traverse

INTERMEDIATE

13.8 miles

The initial part of this trip requires good route-finding skills, and the route is best done from west to east as the meandering course of Cedar Lake Creek can be confusing to navigate. Keep in mind also that this route is point to point. Launch from the boat ramp within the San Bernard National Wildlife Refuge along Cedar Lake Creek. Paddle down the creek and notice the transition from wooded riparian habitat to low coastal marsh. It is approximately 5.6 miles to the intracoastal waterway. The creek meanders increasingly in the last mile. As the waterway opens up into a small lake formed by an old oxbow, stay to the left and look for the small waterway on the other side of this lake that meanders east to the intracoastal waterway. Cross the intracoastal into Cedar Lake #4 and paddle 1.1 miles south-southeast to the Cedar Cut camping area. WARNING! The Cedar Lakes have many shallow oyster reefs that can tear up kayak hulls. If water levels are low, this route is not possible. While paddling south-southeast, stay to the right of Cedar Cut to avoid the shallow reefs and bars. There is a sandy area suitable for camping along the southern corner of Cedar Lake #4 (see map). After camping, paddle back to the intracoastal waterway. On your way you might detour a little to the northwest around the bar—which usually has thousands of sea birds congregating on it—to birdwatch or fish along the drop off. I would encourage paddlers to head back to the intracoastal waterway

rather than try to paddle across Cedar Lake #4 because of the many shallow oyster reefs we encountered. Ken Johnson's remarks as we struggled through a "minefield" of these jagged reefs are unprintable. From the mouth of Cedar Lake #4 adjacent to where Cedar Lake Creek enters the intracoastal waterway, paddle approximately 6 miles to reach the boat ramp at the end of FM 2918 just west of the San Bernard River.

Ken Johnson getting supplies to make breakfast in the early morning light.

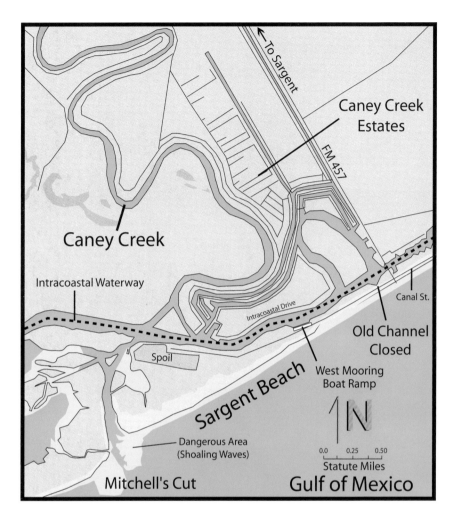

Caney Creek Estates

To Sargent

FM 457

Caney Creek

Intracoastal Waterway

Canal St.

Intracoastal Drive

Old Channel Closed

Spoil

West Mooring Boat Ramp

Sargent Beach

N

0.0   0.25   0.50
Statute Miles

Dangerous Area (Shoaling Waves)

Mitchell's Cut   Gulf of Mexico

 Sargent Beach can best be accessed directly from the beach by more experienced paddlers and by the more protected West Mooring boat ramp along the intracoastal waterway.

▲ *Only a few small commercial fishing boats use Mitchell's Cut near Sargent. The narrow channels are shallow and lined with extensive oyster reefs.*

Sargent Beach and Matagorda Peninsula State Park

ALL SKILL LEVELS

variable mileage

It is unclear where Matagorda Peninsula State Park begins and ends and where Sargent Beach begins, as the area is completely undeveloped and without signage. More advanced paddlers can launch and land along the outer coast from Sargent Beach to Mitchell's Cut in Matagorda Peninsula State Park. However, at Mitchell's Cut there are dangerous shoaling waves offshore to the east. I did discover that the edge of the area of shoaling can be fun to surf with care. For those interested in calm water paddling, fishing, and birding, launch from the West Mooring boat ramp along the intracoastal

waterway. Paddle west along the intracoastal for approximately 1.4 miles and turn southwest into the channel that goes into East Matagorda Bay. If you continue toward the bay, the channel becomes a sand flat with wading birds and is impassable unless there are flood tides. A channel that branches off to the west is also very shallow. There is a small, shallow bay with good fishing to the south of the channel immediately after turning off the intracoastal waterway. Just west of the shallow bay is the channel to Mitchell's Cut. The beaches along the cut are a great place for picnicking and can be good for surfing for more experienced paddlers. Stay to the west of the cut if you wish to avoid unpredictable currents and breaking waves on the adjacent shoals. For those who want a longer trip, the mouth of the Colorado River at Matagorda Bay Nature Park is approximately 22 miles to the southwest along the outer coast.

◀ *Passes form a bottle-neck where fish from adjacent bays or the Gulf of Mexico make easy prey for pelicans.*

▼ *Matagorda Bay Nature Park and East Matagorda Bay along the Colorado River outflow. L indicates launching sites.*

Matagorda Bay Nature Park, Colorado River Mouth, and Outer Coast

INTERMEDIATE TO ADVANCED

variable mileage

Paddlers can launch either from the beach adjacent to the main parking area at the mouth of the Colorado River or from the beach fringing the Gulf of Mexico northeast of the main parking area. When launching from the mouth of the Colorado River, extreme caution should be exercised to avoid fishermen along the pier and breakwater as well as the submerged 10-ton granite blocks that flank the shoreward side of the pier. The blocks are often not visible except at low tide or with breaking waves. During all but extremely calm conditions, paddlers should walk out on the pier or breakwater and observe wave conditions prior to launch. Generally, paddlers launching here should stay on the west side of the channel going into the Gulf of Mexico to avoid dangerous currents and shoaling waves.

For paddlers interested in longer open water trips, it is approximately 19 miles to the Matagorda Ship Channel and an additional 5 miles to Port O'Connor. If open water conditions suddenly become dangerous because of wind or wave action, there are several washover channels along the Matagorda Peninsula that would only require a short portage to reach the calmer waters of Matagorda Bay. To the northeast, Mitchell's Cut is approximately 18.4 miles up the coast.

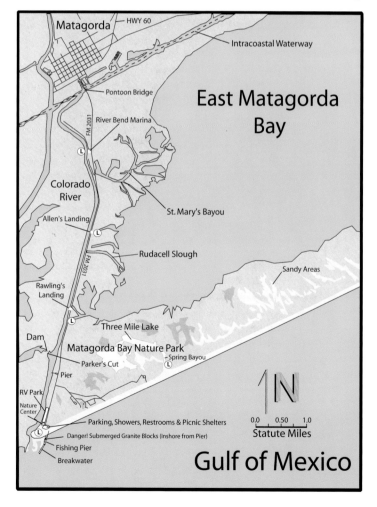

The American oyster-catcher (Haematopus palliates) is a common shoreline resident that feeds primarily on clams and oysters, as its name suggests. Photo by Winifred Shrum

Three Mile Lake

INTERMEDIATE

1–3 miles

This route is possible only when water levels are high, and care must be taken not to get vehicles stuck at the launch site. Pay close attention to prevailing winds and tides, as changes in both may profoundly affect water levels. Launch from the east side of Spring Bayou to enter Three Mile Lake. The wetlands are known for good birdwatching, and many flounder are caught here.

East Matagorda Bay

BEGINNING TO INTERMEDIATE

variable mileage

Launch from the canal south of Rawling's Landing, but be sure to park across the road to the south, where there is a wider shoulder and area suitable for parking. Paddle east down the canal, but be careful to note your position either with GPS or by using the buildings along FM 2031 as a reference, since it is rather easy to get lost in these wetlands. You can paddle through the canal into East Matagorda Bay and follow the south-

ern shoreline. Approximately 2 miles out, the shoreline opens into shallow wetlands. If the tide is high enough, it might be possible to get into Three Mile Lake. However, shallow water and oysters can make this hazardous. If you do venture into this area, make sure you have a good handle on prevailing winds and tides, as these can change water levels quite quickly. These marshy wetlands are excellent for birdwatching and can provide very good fishing for sea trout and redfish, especially in the fall. This canal can also be used to explore the western shore and bayous of East Matagorda Bay.

Colorado River to the Gulf

INTERMEDIATE

5.7–9.1 miles

With four launch sites quite close together, there are several approaches for paddlers exploring the lower reaches of the Colorado River. The first described here goes point to point from the public boat ramp next to the River Bend Restaurant to the Matagorda Bay Nature Park at the mouth of the Colorado River (approximately 5.7 miles). Paddlers should be wary of boat traffic on the river. The eastern shoreline is developed until just south of Rawling's Landing. Expect to see a number of commercial fishing boats. Birdwatching and fishing are usually good, especially at the mouth of the river where it enters the Gulf. Approximately 4 miles from the launch, the river widens along the western shoreline and an earthen dam blocks what once was Parker's Cut. In *Flyfishing the Texas Coast,* Scates and Shook report that it is possible to portage over the earthen dam to fish the deep clear channels and isolated bayous of eastern Matagorda Bay.

The second route involves first paddling north 1.7 miles to the intracoastal waterway pontoon bridge and then turning around to paddle south to the Matagorda Bay Nature Park, to finish at the beach adjacent to the main parking area (approximately 9.1 miles). It is fun to observe some of the workboats and barge traffic and see how the pontoon bridge works along the intracoastal waterway, but be careful to stay out of the way! ■

Matagorda Bay to Northern San Antonio Bay

THE SECTION OF THE Texas coast reaching southward from Matagorda Bay is characterized by extensive areas of oyster reefs and bayshores lined with a combination of marshes and muddy wetlands interspersed with sand and shell beaches. The rainfall and runoff are much higher than in South Texas, and the more turbid bays are more estuarine. The outer coast dunes are generally smaller than farther south. The islands, bays, and bayshores in this area are historically significant and great places to observe wildlife and go fishing.

Matagorda Bay is the site of the ill-fated French expedition led by La Salle from 1684 to 1687. Entrusted with four ships, La Salle was to establish a fortified settlement near the mouth of the Mississippi River. After losing one of his ships to pirates, he landed in Matagorda Bay more than 400 miles west of the Mississippi River. The storeship *Aimable,* carrying most of the colonists' supplies, sank as it entered Matagorda Bay through Cavallo Pass. A third ship took the storeship's crew and some disenchanted colonists back to France. The remaining ship *Belle* capsized in Matagorda Bay during a squall late in

the winter of 1686. Most of those who stayed with the expedition to finish the temporary Fort St. Louis succumbed to dehydration, malnutrition, or overwork or were killed by Indians. La Salle was eventually killed by his own men near the Brazos River. A small group made it to Canada and then returned to France. Later

▼ *Sunset at our camp along Matagorda Bay.*

◀ *It was a bizarre scene. Thousands of fiddler crabs (Uca minax) swarmed out of the marsh over our shell beach and through our camp on Matagorda Bay one night. Females carry developing eggs to the water's edge, where they release their larvae a few days before the next spring tide.*

expeditions rescued a few people from the Indians. The 54-foot *Belle* was found by Texas State Marine Archaeologist J. Barto Arnold in 1995. A special coffer dam was built around the wreck in Matagorda Bay so that the water could be pumped out and the wreck excavated. The mud of Matagorda Bay had preserved the ship and its contents from decay to an amazing extent. An array of artifacts, essentially comprising a seventeenth-century French colonizing kit, were found in good condition. Many of the *Belle*'s artifacts have been placed on display at seven Texas museums.

Paddling along Matagorda Bay, one can only ponder what it might have been like for the early settlers. On the eastern side of the bay are extensive shell beaches from Palacios Point to Coon Island Bay, with a small inlet into Oyster Lake, a large lagoon full of wildlife. When winds are out of the southwest, paddling conditions are challenging and fun for those with experience. Extending from Palacios Point toward the southwest is Halfmoon Reef. In July of 1858 the Halfmoon Reef Lighthouse was mounted on pilings to mark the reef, as it posed a navigational hazard. The small wooden lighthouse is now on display in Port Lavaca adjacent to the Highway 35 causeway. Palacios Point was the original location of the town of Palacios when it was established in 1838. It was moved to its present location on Tres Palacios Bay in 1902. At least one early foundation remains on the point, thought to be the old O'Neal Hotel. This is now a part of Rusty Green's cattle ranch. Much of Oyster Lake and its surrounding marshland is managed by the Nature Conservancy. North of the inlet to Oyster Bay is Oliver Point, which was the original town site for the port of Austin in 1836, also a failed settlement. Just to the north of Oliver Point are Coon Island and Coon Island Bay. The bay is an old ship graveyard and has been used to scuttle ships for more than 150 years. A small tidal creek at the north end of bay is good for birdwatching and fishing.

On the west side of Matagorda Bay is the historic town site of Indianola. Originally Indian Point and a small adjacent German community called Karlshaven grew together and merged to become Indianola in 1849. The town's population had reached nearly five thousand by the time a major hurricane struck in 1875, destroying three-fourths of its buildings and killing hundreds of people. A schooner was washed five miles inland and the storm was estimated to have killed more than fifteen thousand head of livestock. The town was rebuilt, only to be completely destroyed by another hurricane in 1886. The latter storm was so destructive and killed so many residents that the town was abandoned. Paddlers can launch from the Indianola Fishing Marina to explore Powderhorn Lake and Matagorda Bay. Much of the north shore of Powderhorn Lake is occupied by the 3,440-acre Myrtle Foester Whitmire Unit of the Aransas National Wildlife Refuge; this unit was added to the refuge in 1993 and is a good place for birdwatching.

Much of the Port Lavaca area has been industrialized, and Cavallo Pass was no longer adequate for shipping traffic. As a result, the Matagorda Ship Channel now cuts through the Matagorda Island Peninsula and is flanked by jetties. A small bird refuge is located on Bird Island just inside the channel and is worth a visit during the spring. A good rough water trip is to circle out of Cavallo Pass into the Gulf of Mexico and back into the Matagorda Ship Channel. Only intermediate to advanced paddlers should venture here, and only with extreme caution and depending on surf conditions. The shoaling and breaking waves of Cavallo Pass can be dangerous, as the remains of several wrecks attest, including La Salle's ship the *Aimable*.

At Seadrift along the northeastern shore of San Antonio Bay, paddlers can see birds and alligators and fish among huge stands of reeds and the extensive marshland that characterize the Guadalupe River delta. Seadrift was originally known as Lower Mott and was settled by a few Germans who left Karlshaven (later to become Indianola) in 1848. Seadrift's Bayfront Park is hallowed ground for paddlers, as this is the finish for the Texas Water Safari. The grueling endurance race down the Guadalupe River was established in 1963 by Frank Brown and "Big Willie" George, who first paddled a large row boat from San Marcos to Corpus Christi in thirty days in 1962. The modern version traverses 260 miles of rivers and bays from San Marcos to Seadrift, with the fastest recorded finish under thirty hours in 1997.

Beautiful shell beaches and islands that separate San

Antonio Bay from Espiritu Santo Bay can be accessed from Charlie's Bait Camp just southeast of Seadrift. The area is well known for birds and dolphin watching. Flounder fishing is often good in the adjacent Shoalwater Bay. Over the years this area became a popular destination for paddlers thanks to the efforts of Bill Minor of Tide Guide Expeditions from San Antonio. This is a great area for paddlers to camp.

Separating Espiritu Santo Bay and San Antonio Bay from the Gulf of Mexico is the 38-mile-long Matagorda Island, ranging from less than a mile to 4 miles wide. The southwestern end of the island flanking Mesquite Bay is covered in the next section. The island supports large numbers of migratory birds, a white-tailed deer population, feral pigs, coyotes, a variety of small mammals, and alligators. For many years the northern end of the island was managed as a state park, with a ferry taking visitors in along the intracoastal waterway from park headquarters in Port O'Connor. Ferry service was discontinued and the Port O'Connor office was closed on October 31, 2005. The Matagorda Island National Wildlife Refuge and State Natural Area are now jointly operated by the state and the U.S. Fish and Wildlife Service as the Matagorda Island Wildlife Management Area. Established camp sites and island beaches provide excellent fishing and wildlife watching opportunities. Texas Parks and Wildlife maintains paddling trails from Port O'Connor to Matagorda Island.

The island is home to one of the first lighthouses on the Texas Coast. The original lighthouse began operation in 1852 to guide ships through Cavallo Pass into Matagorda Bay to reach Indianola, which for a time became the second busiest port in Texas. After sustaining considerable damage during the Civil War, the lighthouse was rebuilt and relocated to its present site farther inland on Matagorda Island. It was automated in the 1950s and deactivated after falling into disrepair in 1995. Recently rebuilt by the Matagorda Island Foundation, the lighthouse is well worth a visit.

Recommended Navigational Aids

Upper Laguna Madre to San Antonio Bay and *Matagorda Bay* by Hook-N-Line Map Company; aerial maps downloaded from TerraServer (www.terraserver.com),

Google Earth (http://earth.google.com), or MapQuest (www.mapquest.com).

Planning Considerations

For those needing transportation to and from Matagorda Island, there are a number of qualified and reputable guides available at Port O'Connor (www.texas saltwaterfishing.com/portoconnor/). As with most of the bays, try to avoid low tides, especially when paddling Lucas Lake, Powderhorn Lake, Coon Island Bay, Shoalwater Bay, Pringle Lake, and Oyster Lake. Beware of oyster reefs. There is a $5 fee for parking and the use of the beach and boat ramps at Charlie's Bait Camp (www.charliesbait.com) and the Indianola Fishing Center.

A cell phone is usually adequate for emergencies. Be prepared to call the Port O'Connor Coast Guard Station at 512–983–2617 for emergencies.

Accommodations

Primitive camping is allowed at Shell Bar/Steamboat Island, on the Matagorda Peninsula adjacent to the Matagorda Ship Channel jetties, and on Matagorda Island, Coon Island, and a shell beach adjacent to Oyster Lake on Matagorda Bay. Matagorda Island has established bayside campsites with restroom facilities and an outdoor shower near the abandoned airport on the northeast end of the island. I prefer to camp nearby on Sunday Beach to avoid mosquitoes and have a nice onshore breeze during the warmer months. Camping is also allowed along the outer coast beaches on Matagorda Island. There are many options for accommodations in Seadrift, Port O'Connor, and Port Lavaca (www.coastalbendtexas.com). The best hotel in Seadrift is Robbie Gregory's Captain's Quarters (361-785-4982), and the company also has a hotel in Port O'Connor (361-983-4982). The old Port Motel in Port O'Connor is almost within walking distance from the boat ramps at the Fishing Center (361-983-2724, portmotel@ portmotel.com). At Powderhorn Lake, the Indianola Fishing Marina allows tent camping and has RV sites and small cabins for rent (361-552-5350, www.indiano lafishingmarina.com). Other nearby accommodations are at Magnolia Beach (www.magnoliavacation.com). For those visiting the eastern side of Matagorda Bay accommodations are available at Palacios (361-972-2615, www.palacioschamber.com).

Directions to Launch Sites

Eastern Matagorda Bay Shoreline: Turn east on FM 521 off Highway 35 approximately 3.5–4 miles north of Palacios. Pass the Palacios River and Carl's Park and then turn south on FM 1095. After FM 1095 takes a sharp right turn, turn left on CR 378/Brazos Tower Road. Travel south and turn right on CR 373/Franzen Road. Drive a short distance west to CR 365/Oyster Lake Road. Follow Oyster Lake Road south past a shrimp farm and eventually over a small bridge that crosses the inlet into Oyster Lake from Matagorda Bay. After the road crosses the bridge, it ends at a locked gate. To the right is an oyster shell beach along Matagorda Bay. Camping is permitted from the ranch boundary to the Oyster Lake bridge along Matagorda Bay. Kayakers can park and launch from this shoreline. If you want to paddle to Coon Island, there is a small unmarked road just north of the Oyster Lake bridge that also goes down to the shoreline, where you can park and launch.

Powderhorn Lake: To launch or land at the western end of Powderhorn Lake, drive south on Highway 185 from Victoria or from the Highway 35 junction to Seadrift. Continue on Highway 185 east approximately 10–11 miles to reach FM 1289 north. Turn left on FM 1289 and drive about 4–5 miles north to the bridge that crosses a small salt creek connecting Coloma Lake with Powderhorn Lake. To reach Powderhorn Lake, paddle north from the bridge.

To access the eastern side of Powderhorn Lake, drive to Indianola Fishing Marina (361-552-5350, www.indianolafishingmarina.com). From Victoria or from Highway 59, take Highway 87 southeast. Turn right on FM 2433 just south of the small town of Kamey. Cross Highway 35 and continue south to Highway 238. Turn right on Highway 238 and continue south. Turn left on FM 316 until you reach Ocean Drive along Matagorda Bay. Follow Ocean Drive past the La Salle Monument (a 22-foot-tall granite marker) until it ends at the Indianola Fishing Marina. There is a $5 charge for use of the boat ramp.

Port O'Connor: To reach Matagorda Island Peninsula or Matagorda Island from Port O'Connor, continue east on Highway 185 from Seadrift until you reach Port O'Connor. To launch at the Fishing Center (361-983-4440, www.pocfishingcenter.com), turn right on 15th Street and drive until it dead ends into Water Street. Turn left to reach the marina and boat ramps. There is currently a $3 charge to use the boat ramp. You can also launch from the beach park along Matagorda Bay. To reach the park, continue on Highway 185 until it dead ends on Park Street. Turn left and the park is on the right. The launch here is very shallow. For multiday trips I prefer to leave my vehicle at the Port Motel and launch at the nearby boat ramp.

Charlie's Bait Camp: To access Steamboat Island and Shell Bar, continue east past Seadrift on Highway 185. About 4–5 miles east, look for Lane Road and a weathered sign for Charlie's Bait Camp. Turn south on Lane Road and drive south until you reach a small settlement along the intracoastal waterway. Turn right or southwest on Welder Flats Road a short distance to reach the parking area, boat ramp, and beach at Charlie's Bait Camp (361–785–3023, www.charliesbait.com). Parking is $5 per day and there is a $5 fee to launch from the beach or boat ramp. Kayakers normally launch from the beach.

Seadrift's Bayfront Park: Travel southeast on Highway 185 from Victoria or from the intersection with Highway 35 to get to Seadrift. In Seadrift, turn right

Side Trip
The Palacios Area Historical Association operates the Palacios Museum in the Hill Building, a 1910 mercantile building, where you may see some of the artifacts from La Salle's 1685 expedition (361-972-5241). Bird enthusiasts can view whooping cranes and other interesting wildlife at the Aransas National Wildlife Refuge on boat charters from Rockport or Port Aransas (Pisces Charters: 800–245–9324; The Skimmer: 877-892-4737, www.whoopingcrane tours.com; and the Wharf Cat, Rockport 800782–2473, www.wharfcat.com, Port Aransas 800-605-5448).

on South Main Street. Drive down to the end of South Main Street and turn right on West Bay Avenue along the water to get to Bayfront Park. You will pass a flag pole and the sign for the finish of the Texas Water Safari. At the west end of the park is a seldom used boat ramp and dirt parking lot that kayakers can use to access the Guadalupe River delta.

Oyster Lake/Palacios Point Loop

INTERMEDIATE
11.5 miles

Starting from the camping area on the oyster shell beach, paddle north around the small spit and into the inlet to Oyster Bay. Paddle under the bridge and directly 0.25 mile into the bay to avoid shell reefs that flank the inlet. Now paddle about 0.75 mile southeast across the bay toward the nearest point of land along the southern shore of Oyster Lake. This is actually an island, as you will soon discover. Follow the beautifully vegetated mud bluff southeast. As you pass the east end of the island, you will see an inlet through an oyster reef that goes in behind the island. If the tide is high enough, there are often many fish in the channel behind the island. The channel gets too shallow to circumnavigate the island.

As you paddle along Oyster Lake's southern shore you will see two separate pilings. Stay to the outside of these pilings to avoid oyster reefs. The marsh in this area is a good place to watch birds. After paddling approximately 2.4 miles along the shoreline, you will see a large navigational piling at the entrance to the Gulf Intracoastal Waterway. There are automated lights and a sign on the piling with a large #2. Paddle out of Oyster Lake into the intracoastal waterway going southwest. In the distance is a series of large buoys lining the south side of the waterway. These are mooring buoys for barge traffic if conditions are too rough to cross Matagorda Bay. Two miles from the outlet of Oyster Lake, the intracoastal waterway opens into Matagorda Bay. At the end of the spoil island is a sand spit where kayakers can land to rest and get a good view of the bay from the low bluff above the beach. This is also a place where people commonly camp. There are often dolphins frequenting this area and very good birdwatching and fishing.

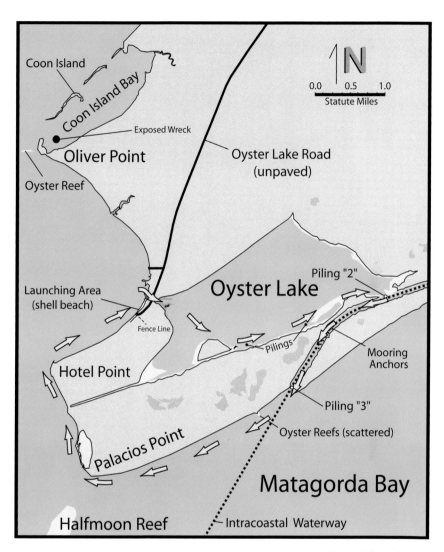

▲ Oyster Lake and Coon Island Bay along the eastern Matagorda Bay shoreline. The arrows indicate the Oyster Lake–Palacios Point loop.

◀ Lush vegetation lines Oyster Lake near Palacios.

▶ An old oil industry "crew boat" sits rusting in the shallows of Coon Island Bay, a graveyard for ships since the 1800s. Photo by Ken Johnson

▲ A monument dedicated to French explorer La Salle who landed in Matagorda Bay in 1684. His ship the Belle was discovered in this bay by Texas State Marine Archaeologist J. Barto Arnold in 1995, and many of the artifacts are on display at several Texas museums.

Make sure you secure your boats! Last time I was there Ken Johnson and I almost had our boats washed out into Matagorda Bay. We were resting on a log watching dolphins splashing about when a barge approached from the east along the intracoastal. The tugboat's propellers pushed water back up the channel. As the boat approached, the water receded. After the barge passed us we were engulfed by a small tsunami that swept our boats from the shoreline. Fortunately, Ken was able to catch both before they were washed into Matagorda Bay.

From the mouth of the intracoastal waterway, paddle slightly less than 3.5 miles along the shoreline to Palacios Point. These low grassy bluffs are part of a private cattle ranch. You may see the remains of an old windmill about halfway down the shore. Be careful of some scattered oyster reefs extending from the shoreline. As you round Palacios Point, there is a sandy/shell strand flanking a small salt lagoon. Occasionally a small inlet opens during storm activity. There are many birds here and beautiful shell beaches with stunted trees and scattered prickly pear cacti. From the salt lagoon around Hotel Point back to the launching area is a large concentration of salt cedar or tamarisk bushes lining the shell beaches.

Coon Island Bay

INTERMEDIATE
10–11 miles

Launch from either the shell beach south of the Oyster Lake inlet bridge or from the end of the road that goes to the shoreline just north of the bridge. The latter is preferable as it shortens the roundtrip distance by about 1 mile. Starting from the unmarked road north

of the bridge, paddle less than 2.5 miles northwest around Oliver Point. From here it is difficult to see Coon Island. Paddle north from the point about 0.25 mile. From this perspective you should be able to see a low oyster shell strand that extends northeast. Stay to the left along the seaward side of the strand for another 0.25 miles and you will see a small sandy/shell island with vegetation and a large log to sit on. Camping is permitted here. Numerous birds usually line the narrow shell/sand strands adjacent to the islands. Fishing is good here and in the small bay behind the island. Just north of Coon Island paddle northeast into Coon Island Bay. At the northeastern corner of the bay is a small oak motte or thicket that is slightly elevated. Paddle 1.25 miles toward the thicket. To the left is a small tidal creek good for fishing and birdwatching. After this side trip, paddle to the bluffs along the southern shore of Coon Island Bay about 1.5 miles. From here you may see the recent wreck of an oil company crew boat toward Oliver Point. Paddle 0.5 mile west to Oliver Point and 2.5 miles back to the launch area.

Powderhorn Lake/ Western Matagorda Bay

BEGINNING TO INTERMEDIATE
1–13 miles

This is one of the most historic places on the Texas coast. Plaques tell the tragic story of Indianola and how the second largest port in Texas was completely destroyed by hurricanes. A large monument is dedicated to the French explorer La Salle, who landed in this bay in 1685. Just past this park on South Ocean Drive are the Indianola Fishing Center and a boat ramp where kayakers can conveniently launch. Paddlers can

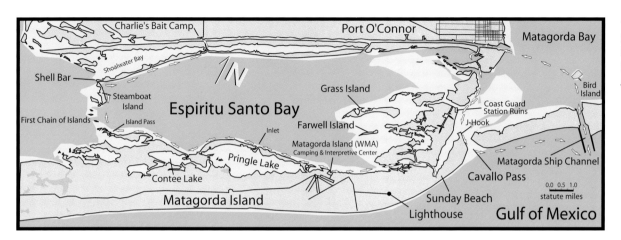

◄ Eastern Matagorda Island and Espíritu Santo Bay. The arrows indicate the Cavallo Pass–Matagorda Island loop.

wander northwest or southeast along Matagorda Bay to fish and watch birds or paddle into Powderhorn Lake. Powderhorn Lake is a popular area for fishing, duck hunting, and birdwatching. It also adjoins the Whitmore Unit, a disjunct part of the Aransas National Wildlife Refuge.

If entering Powderhorn Lake, stay left to avoid the extensive oyster reefs at the mouth of the lake. After you are well into the lake, paddle about 1.5 miles west past a residential area along the north shore. As you paddle southwest along the shoreline, you are seeing the shore of the Whitmore Unit, a poorly known part of the Aransas NWR. About a mile farther down the shoreline is a miniature breakwater protecting a habitat restoration area. This is a great place for birdwatching.

Paddlers interested in a one-way trip (6.5–7 miles) can paddle around the lake and exit through a marshy channel along the southwestern shore of the lake. It is only about 0.5–0.6 mile down the channel to the FM 1289 bridge. Alternatively, during times when the wind is from the southwest, this trip is easier in reverse from the Fm 1289 bridge to the Indianola Fishing Center.

For those finishing the loop around Powderhorn Lake (13 miles), paddle approximately 4 miles along the southern shoreline and you will see an abandoned oil company docking facility. Continue paddling along the Powderhorn Ranch shoreline about a mile before turning due north to the Indianola Fishing Center. Again, be careful to find the channel because of the extensive oyster reefs at the mouth of Powderhorn Lake.

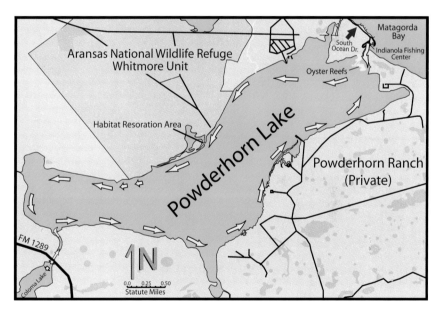

▲ Powderhorn Lake with the Whitmire Unit of the Aransas National Wildlife Refuge along the northern shoreline. This lake is just south of the abandoned town of Indianola, which was once the second largest port in Texas.

Cavallo Pass/Matagorda Ship Channel Loop

INTERMEDIATE TO ADVANCED WITH SURF EXPERIENCE
17–18 miles

This route should be approached with extreme caution and only during calm weather. Even advanced paddlers with surf experience should not undertake this trip when wind and waves are significant or during bad weather. Cavallo Pass can be very dangerous as it has shoaling, breaking waves, and strong currents.

The Matagorda Ship Channel provides a much safer entrance into the bay than Cavallo Pass. The jetties flanking the pass are good for fishing, and the protected beaches provide a safe haven for kayakers.

To begin this trip follow the instructions on the Sunday Beach route to get to J-Hook. If the water is rough on the way to J-Hook, it is probably too rough to paddle through Cavallo Pass. From the sand spit at J-Hook, paddle east across Cavallo Pass. Before entering the Gulf of Mexico, land on the northeast side of the pass to survey areas of shoaling and observe wave sets to ensure safety. There are several wrecks in and around the pass that also may pose hazards. Usually it is best to stay left as you exit the pass to avoid rough water. Paddle about 4.5 miles northeast along the shoreline and out around the jetty to enter the Matagorda Ship Channel. Avoid ship traffic by paddling north along the west side of the channel. On the north side of the south jetty is a sheltered beach good for landing and camping.

Paddle 2 miles north through the remainder of the ship channel through the Matagorda Peninsula to Bird Island, where birdwatching is especially good during the spring. Landing is not permitted here. Turn west and paddle 3 miles across the bay to reach the intracoastal waterway behind Port O'Connor to finish the trip back at the Fishing Center.

Matagorda Island Wildlife Management Area

INTERMEDIATE TO ADVANCED

18–19 miles

Formerly there was a state park office in Port O'Connor along the intracoastal waterway, with parking, boat ramps, and a small ferry used to transport tourists to Matagorda Island. However, due to statewide budget cuts the facility was closed in 2005 and the state has changed the island's designation from state park to wildlife management area. To paddle to the island now, launch from the boat ramps at the Fishing Center in Port O'Connor and paddle south through the small cut into Barroom Bay. Do not paddle directly across the bay, but follow the channel markers right and then around to the left to avoid the shallow bar in the middle of the bay. This channel is very narrow and often has a good deal of powerboat traffic. It is wise to paddle just outside these markers. Take the cut on the southeast side of Barroom Bay and continue southeast. You may see the TPWD kayak trail GPS markers here (#2 and #3).

After passing through the cut on the southeast side of Barroom Bay, you have two choices, depending on skill level and weather conditions. To take the more protected route (9 miles), paddle southwest across the Big Bayou to another small cut, where you may see the TPWD kayak trail marker #4, and paddle about 1.5 miles southwest along the Bayucos Island shoreline to reach Mitchell's Cut, where you may see trail markers #6 and #7 as you paddle through (see map). Turn southwest and paddle about a mile down Saluria Bayou. To take the less protected route (9.5 miles), paddle southeast from the cut out of Barroom Bay out of Big Bayou along the eastern shoreline of Bayucos Island for approximately 1.75 miles. This is often choppy and fun for intermediate to more advanced paddlers when winds are out of the east or southeast. You will see the ruins of the old Coast Guard station marking the entrance to Saluria Bayou. The structure is in poor condition, so be careful when exploring. In the 1990s you could stand on top of the structure and get a good view of the island. Beware in June and December when tidal currents in and out of Saluria Bayou can be

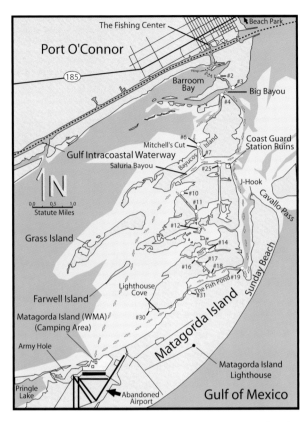

▲ Port O'Connor and northeast Matagorda Island. Numbered GPS markers have been placed to help guide paddlers. The arrows indicate routes to Sunday Beach and the Matagorda Island Wildlife Management Area camp on the back of the island.

▲ Camping on Matagorda Island near Port O'Connor.

strong. Turn west into Saluria Bayou and paddle about 1.75 miles to reach the bay.

As you exit Saluria Bayou, continue southwest about 1 mile to Grass Island. Stay to the left of the island and continue less than a mile to Farwell Island. Again, stay to the left of the island. When you pass Farwell Island, continue southwest 2.5 miles to reach the established campsites on the bay side of Matagorda Island. You will be able to see the cluster of buildings on the horizon that marks the park. Inexperienced paddlers should beware, as this crossing is often rough when winds are from the south. The park camp is a large grassy area with tent sites, picnic tables, a bathroom, and a primitive shower. Many paddlers camp here and paddle to Pringle Lake and Army Hole to the west to fish and birdwatch. Others paddle northeast through Lighthouse Cove and a small salt creek to "the Fish Pond" to reach Sunday Beach and camp.

Army Hole/Pringle Lake

BEGINNING

1 to 8 miles

At one time the University of Texas Outdoor Adventure Program led by Dar Vojdani and other groups and individuals used the state park's ferry to transport paddlers to the camping area on the island, where they explored the old lighthouse and paddled along the back of the island to watch wildlife and go fishing. Now paddlers must either hire a local guide to deliver them to the island (www.texassaltwaterfishing.com/portoconnor/) or paddle there from Port O'Connor (see preceding route).

Two popular destinations from the Matagorda Island bayside camping area are Army Hole and Pringle Lake. Army Hole was actually a small harbor that was dredged to provide cargo ships access to the old military base. It is now an excellent place to go fishing. To access the small cove, paddle east-southeast along the shoreline less than half a mile and you will find the small inlet. At times this is also a good place to watch birds. Pringle Lake is another good destination for fishing and birding. To reach the lake continue paddling

A flock of American avocet (Recurvirostra americana) along the shoreline behind Matagorda Island. Their upcurved bill is moved quickly from side to side in shallow water or mud to trap tiny food items.

east along the shoreline past Army Hole approximately 3 more miles. At the mouth of the inlet to Pringle Lake is a large sandy beach that makes a convenient rest stop. The lake is not very accessible during low tides. Fishermen report great fishing here during November and December.

Sunday Beach

INTERMEDIATE
12.5 miles

Sunday Beach is a popular spot to camp. This is a great trip that allows intermediate paddlers with limited surf experience to access the outer coast dune fields without paddling in the open Gulf of Mexico or through the rough waters of Cavallo Pass. Besides seeing outer coast sand dune communities, paddlers get to see marshland and bayshore ecosystems as well.

To start the trip, launch from the boat ramps at the Fishing Center in Port O'Connor and paddle south through the small cut into Barroom Bay. Follow the channel markers right and then around to the left to avoid the shallow bar in the middle of the bay. This channel is narrow and it is wise to paddle just outside these markers to avoid boat traffic. Take the cut on the southeast side of Barroom Bay and continue southeast. You may see the TPWD kayak trail GPS markers #2 and #3 here.

From the cut out of Barroom Bay, paddle out of Big Bayou along the eastern shoreline of Bayucos Island

for approximately 1.75 miles. This is often choppy and fun for intermediate to more advanced paddlers when winds are out of the east or southeast. You will see the ruins of the old Coast Guard station marking the entrance to Saluria Bayou. The structure is in poor condition, so be careful when exploring. In the 1990s, you could stand on top of the structure and get a good view of the island. Beware in June and December when tidal currents in and out of Saluria Bayou can be strong. From the old Coast Guard station ruins, it is less than a mile to J-Hook, the sandy spit just inside Cavallo Pass. The sandy spit is a good place to rest en route to Sunday Beach. From the sandy spit, it is a protected 2-mile paddle south to the sandy shore behind Sunday Beach.

A number of side trips are possible from here. Many fisherman and wildlife enthusiasts paddle back into "the Fish Pond" and adjacent tidal creeks. I have paddled up behind deer swimming across the tidal creek that extends northwest from the Fish Pond. If you paddle the salt creek that winds southwest from the Fish Pond, you can access Lighthouse Cove and the Matagorda Island bayside camping area (approximately 5 miles). Less than a mile before you reach the camping area is a road that allows people access to the Matagorda Island Lighthouse (described in the introduction to the section). It is approximately a 2.25-mile hike from the shoreline to reach the lighthouse (see map). The lighthouse makes an excellent navigational marker for kayakers as it can be seen from a great distance.

Shell Bar/Steamboat Island Loop

BEGINNING TO INTERMEDIATE

11–15 miles

Launch from the beach at Charlie's Bait Camp on the intracoastal waterway. Paddle northeast for a short distance before turning southeast along the cut that enters Espiritu Santo Bay. At approximately 0.75 mile from the beach launching area is the open expanse of Espiritu Santo Bay. Turn southwest along the marshy shoreline and paddle slightly less than 5 miles more to reach the narrow pass between Steamboat Island and Shell Bar. Kayakers camp on Shell Bar on the north side and the eastern shell beach along Steamboat Island on the south side of the small pass. The oyster shell beaches are ideal for camping. Kayakers staying at either location often paddle southeast to explore the First Chain of Islands or paddle through Island Pass to explore South Pass Lake as a side trip. There is good bird watching and fishing here. I have occasionally seen whooping cranes here and along the intracoastal waterway nearby. Another good side trip is into Shoalwater Bay, where the fishing is often good. Dolphins commonly congregate at Shell Bar and can be most entertaining. Normally we make the trip into a loop by paddling past Shell Bar into San Antonio Bay and following the shoreline due west to the intracoastal waterway, which leads back to Charlie's Bait Camp. It is less than 3 miles to the intracoastal and about 6.5–7 miles back along it to Charlie's. A shorter loop for the more adventurous is to paddle around the tip of Shell Bar and north into Shoalwater Bay about 1 mile. At this point, you should see a row of pilings oriented northwest. Turn left in front of the pilings and paddle northwest less than 0.5 mile. At one time there was a small cut here that has since filled in with sand. Kayakers can portage about 200 feet across the sandy area to access the intracoastal waterway. Across the intracoastal you will see a small ranch house, and farther northeast along the intracoastal are a couple of small lagoons with good birding and fishing. I have seen whooping cranes during the winter in this area. This portage

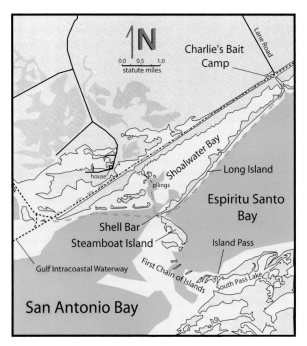

Shell Bar and Steamboat Island. The arrows indicate the typical route from Charlie's Bait Camp. The route can be shortened considerably by paddling through Shoalwater Bay and portaging over to the intracoastal waterway.

shortens the loop by about 4 miles. Bill Minor of Tide Guide Expeditions in San Antonio is an excellent guide and source of information for this area.

Another option is to paddle from Steamboat Island or Shell Bar past Pringle Lake to reach the established campsites on the bay side of Matagorda Island (approximately 11 miles) to camp for the night before heading to Port O'Connor (9 miles) to end the trip.

Guadalupe River Delta/Lucas Lake Loop

INTERMEDIATE

8–10 miles

Launch from the public boat ramp at the western end of Bayfront Park in Seadrift (see Directions to Launch Sites). This is not a good route during low tides! Paddle 3–3.5 miles west to reach Grassy Point. Watch for ship traffic as you cross the Victoria Barge Canal. Along the way you will pass some small oyster shell islands covered in giant reeds 8–12 feet high. Beware of oysters. As you approach Grassy Point, you will see more of these reeds rising above the water. Much of the Guadalupe River delta is covered in these tall reeds and a variety of grasses. Most stands are the common reed

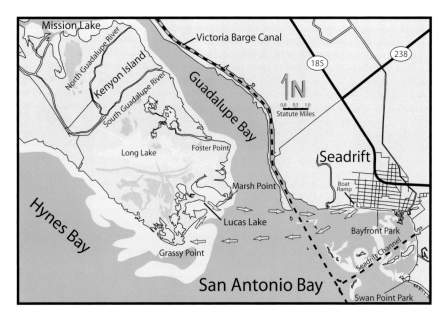

(*Phragmites australis*), which can tolerate the brackish waters where rivers and streams enter the bays. If you see areas where the reeds have been knocked down, watch for alligators, as there are many in this area. Paddle northeast along the shoreline until you see the opening to Lucas Lake, where you will find good fishing and often good birdwatching. Continue along the shoreline toward Marsh Point before turning east back to Seadrift. ◼

◀ *The Guadalupe River delta and Seadrift. Launch from Seadrift Park* (L), *which is where the finish of the famous Texas Water Safari is located.*

▲ *Near the mouth of the Guadalupe River are large, dense stands of the common reed* (Phragmites australis), *up to twelve feet tall.*

Goose Island State Park and Aransas National Wildlife Refuge

This is one of the healthiest coastal habitats and most biologically diverse areas of the entire coast. It is an incredible place for paddlers to visit. Rich assemblages of plants and animals can be seen from the ancient sand dune cliffs and wind-sculpted oak mottes along San Antonio Bay, the salt marshes lining the tidal flats of Mustang Lake, and the barrier island dune communities along the Gulf of Mexico. The sands of the Blackjack Peninsula are a remnant of the 120,000-year-old Ingleside Barrier, where remnants of mastodons, mammoths, saber-toothed tigers and even camels have been discovered. Navigating around the Blackjack Peninsula through a maze of low cactus-covered islands with shell beaches and jagged oyster reefs in the bays can be a difficult but very rewarding experience for those interested in quietly observing a whooping crane feeding; reeling in a large redfish is another possibility. Those interested in seeing the more remote places the area has to offer can paddle through the bays and Cedar Bayou to camp among sand dunes and a shipwreck along the shore of the Gulf of Mexico.

Goose Island State Park and the Aransas National Wildlife Refuge occupy parts of the Lamar and Blackjack peninsulas and Matagorda Island just north of Aransas Bay and the towns of Rockport and Fulton. Goose Island State Park was acquired by obtaining deeds from private

Goose Island State Park and surroundings offer a rich assemblage of plants and animals.

land owners between 1931 and 1935. Although the park consists of only a little over 300 acres, the Aransas NWR has grown to include more than 60,000 acres on the mainland and 56,500 acres on Matagorda Island. While the Texas General Land Office and the U.S. Fish and Wildlife Service jointly own the island, Matagorda Island Wildlife Management Area on the northern end is managed by Texas Parks and Wildlife for public use. About 3,000 acres of the Calhoun Peninsula adjacent to Powderhorn Lake was added to the Aransas NWR in 1993 and is discussed earlier with Matagorda Island Wildlife Management Area.

The large Aransas refuge was founded in 1937, in part to save the endangered whooping crane. At that time all of the King Ranch migrants were gone, and there were only eighteen birds remaining in the Blackjack Peninsula population. By 1941 there were only fifteen birds in the population. Interestingly, this low point corresponded with the construction of the intracoastal waterway through their habitat. Thanks to intensive conservation efforts, in May of 2009 there were about 247 birds on the refuge, and more than 532 birds in the wild and captivity, according to the International Whooping Crane

Recovery Team (www.operationmigration.org). A number of other endangered or threatened birds, mammals, and reptiles that appear on the federal and state lists occur in and around the refuge, including the reddish egret, Botteri's sparrow, brown pelican, southern bald eagle, peregrine falcon, aplomado falcon, wood stork, jaguarundi, several sea turtle species, the American alligator, Texas horned lizard, and Texas scarlet snake. At the end of the nineteenth century and beginning of the twentieth, not only were birds being slaughtered for their feathers, but alligators were taken for their skins. When the cattle industry moved north and the dockside beef canneries declined along the Texas Coastal Bend, people began harvesting and processing green sea turtles to produce canned meat and soup. In their book *Aransas: A Naturalist's Guide,* McAlister and McAlister report that in 1890 a Fulton cannery processed more than 250,000 pounds of turtle meat.

Although Matagorda Island and San Jose Island are sometimes separated by Cedar Bayou, they can generally be thought of as one island approximately 61 miles long, separated from the mainland by Cavallo Pass to the north and Aransas Pass to the south. Unlike all other barrier islands along the Texas coast, these islands have almost no human development. Although the private owners of San Jose Island maintain a small ranch there, the old Liberty Airport with the house and pilot's quarters has become the domain of park rangers and researchers. The old lighthouse and old military runways on the northern end of the island have been abandoned. Other habitations that once existed have been swept away by hurricanes. You can only get to the islands by sea or air. This stands in stark contrast to the extensive development on South Padre Island at Port Isabel and just north of the Padre Island National Seashore near Corpus Christi. In addition, the national seashore's beach has become a highway racetrack for careless fishermen in a hurry to get to Mansfield Pass. With this kind of disruption along the outer coast, it is no wonder that efforts to reestablish these beaches as nesting grounds for the severely endangered Kemp's ridley sea turtle have met with only limited success.

Launching and landing kayaks from the main refuge is not permitted. Kayakers are limited to launch-

▼ *Cedar Bayou from the dunes where camping is allowed.*

ing from Goose Island State Park on the southwest side of the refuge on Aransas Bay and Hopper's Landing on the northwest side of the refuge on San Antonio Bay. You can also camp at both places. One of my favorite multiday trips is from Goose Island to Hopper's Landing with an overnight stay on the outer coast at the end of Cedar Bayou. There is a public boat ramp where kayakers can launch or land behind Goose Island to access Aransas Bay. Part of Goose Island State Park includes the "Big Tree," a coastal live oak thought to be over a thousand years old. The tree is more than 35 feet in circumference, approximately 44 feet high, with a maximum crown spread of 90 feet. Just a few hundred feet east of the tree is a public boat ramp on St. Charles Bay where paddlers can also launch. This bay provides paddlers with extensive tidal flats and salt marshes, a few alligators, and great birdwatching and fishing.

Hopper's Landing is less than 3 miles north of the Aransas NWR entrance off FM 2040. It was established by Bob and Flora Hopper in 1940 as a beer joint and dance hall. At that time they built their own skiffs and rented cane poles to tourists for a dollar a day. During the height of the oil boom in the 1950s the family turned to oil field support services and shrimping. They also sold crushed oyster shell for a dredging company from the 1960s to the 1980s. Carlton and Nada Hopper bought the place in 1970 and are currently watching their great-grandchildren growing up at the landing. In the 1990s they returned to catering to tourists. They still have a small store and grill in the old dance hall, not to mention many interesting artifacts and photographs lining the walls of the charming old place. You never know what you might see along their long sand and shell beach. On my first trip I was walking along the shore when what I thought was a large piece of driftwood turned into an alligator skittering down the beach into the water!

Recommended Navigational Aids

Upper Laguna Madre to San Antonio Bay by Hook-N-Line Map Company; aerial maps downloaded from TerraServer (www.terraserver.com), Google Earth (http://earth.google.com), or MapQuest (www .mapquest.com).

Planning Considerations

As you should in many Texas bays, try to avoid low tides when paddling. Realize that the campsite at the end of Cedar Bayou is not accessible at extreme low tides. Also, tidal currents at low tide can be strong in San Carlos Bay, especially during strong north winds. When traveling through San Carlos Bay, try to follow

The trawler God's Gift lived up to that name when her crew drove her high onto the shore near Cedar Bayou during a storm.

Mrs. Hopper at the counter of their historic bar and café. The old building was a dancehall and club in 1940 and must be seen by those using Hopper's Landing.

the large navigational pilings. What looks like open water in this area is often a complex of shallow, jagged oyster reefs.

If you are planning to paddle between Goose Island and Hopper's Landing, consider calling the reliable Captain Sally (361-205-0624, www.captainsally.com) in Rockport to help arrange transportation or to shuttle vehicles between the put-in and take-out. The people at Hopper's landing may also help make such arrangements.

A cell phone is usually adequate for emergencies. Be prepared to call the Port Aransas Coast Guard Station (361-749-5217), or the rangers at Goose Island State Park (361-729-2858) or the Aransas National Wildlife Refuge (361-286-3559) for emergencies. If you have an emergency in Mesquite Bay or Cedar Bayou and you are unable to call for help, there is usually a ranger stationed at Liberty Airport on Matagorda Island who can provide assistance. There is a boat landing on the eastern shore of Mesquite Bay with an adjacent road that goes to the airport.

Accommodations

Goose Island State Park has campsites on and off the island with restroom facilities and showers. My preference is to stay out on the seaward side of the island, where south winds off Aransas Bay help keep the mosquitoes away. RV and tent camping are available at both Goose Island State Park (361-729-2858, www.tpwd.state .tx.us) and Hopper's Landing (361-286-3331 or 286-3126, www.HoppersLanding.com). Hopper's Landing also has small cottages for rent. Other accommodations in this area are too numerous to list, but contact the Chamber of Commerce for Rockport/Fulton (361-729-6445, http://www.rockport-fulton.org/).

Directions to Launch Sites

Hopper's Landing: If you want to launch on San Antonio Bay, travel about 20 miles north of Rockport on Highway 35 until you see the sign for the Aransas National Wildlife Refuge. Turn right on FM 774 at the sign and drive about 8–9 miles, and turn right or southeast on FM 2040 toward the refuge. Look for a small weathered sign that marks the short road to Hopper's Land-

ing on the left, less than 4 miles down the road. When you arrive, let the family know you are present and let them direct you where to launch and park. We usually drive down to the beach on the grass past the outdoor shower stall to unload the boats and equipment and then park in the lot above.

Goose Island State Park: The park is located off Highway 35 just north of Rockport and Fulton across the LBJ Causeway. Turn east on Park Road 13 at the Goose Island State Park sign. You will drive through a grove of beautiful wind-stunted live oaks. When you reach the intersection, a sign indicates the main park to your right and the Big Tree to the left. If you want to launch into Aransas Bay, take a right turn and enter the state park. Just before the bridge onto Goose Island there is a public boat ramp on the left where you can park and launch. Many people also launch from the seaward side of Goose Island. If you want to see St. Charles Bay, then turn left at the intersection and follow Park Road 13 and the signs to the Big Tree. Just down the road from the tree is a public boat ramp on St. Charles Bay.

San Antonio Bay Shoreline

BEGINNING TO INTERMEDIATE
up to 15 miles

The western shoreline of San Antonio Bay is shallow and sandy, with a few scattered oyster reefs. The sandy bluffs and sand dune cliffs are lined with wind-sculpted oak and red bay trees that form dense mottes, especially along the Aransas National Wildlife Refuge. Some of the best examples are around Dagger Point. To access the area, launch from the beach at Hopper's Landing. If you intend paddling close to shore toward the refuge for a few miles, then launch at high tides only because of the shallow water. If you wish to see Dagger Point and McMullen Lake (off limits when whooping cranes are present in the winter), then paddle about 0.5 mile offshore before turning south for about 3 miles. You will see a small oil/gas platform ahead and a smaller well to your right toward shore. You will reach the small platform at nearly 4 miles. Turn southwest and paddle toward Dagger Point. You will see a ribbon of oyster reef trailing off toward Dagger Point at lower tides. Follow Dagger Point Reef

toward Dagger Point. You will notice a stairway down the sandy bluff just south of the point that marks the Dagger Point Trail at the Aransas NWR. You can land here only if you can obtain special permission from the park staff beforehand to explore the oak–red bay mottes that are unique to this area. If you paddle farther south along the shore, you will see the bird observation tower overlooking McMullen Lake. Whooping cranes are present during the winter months. Paddle around the point and into McMullen Lake only if there are no whooping cranes present on the refuge. It is best to obtain permission from park staff first and obey all posted signs on the refuge. Return the way you came, watching for oyster reefs. Usually the prevailing wind makes the trip out slow, but surfing on the way back is fun.

▲ *The sand dune bluffs at Dagger Point can be seen for miles. A stairway up the bluff gives access to the wind-sculpted mottes above. These dense thickets, primarily oak and red bay trees, provide shelter for a variety of wildlife.*

◄ *The cactus-covered island next to the Ayres Dugout along the Second Chain of Islands on our way into Mesquite Bay.*

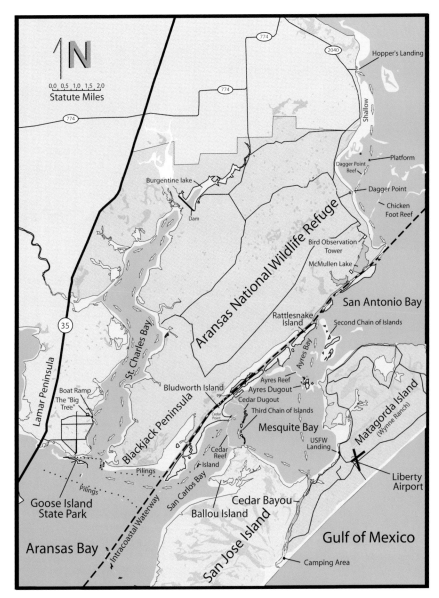

Make sure you are wearing gloves. Associated with the oysters you may find several different kinds of snails, including one of their major predators called the oyster drill. Oyster shells are often covered with small barnacles, the calcareous tubes of serpulid polychaete worms, slipper shells, and occasionally mussels or a sea anemone. The reefs provide food and shelter for a variety of small fish, crabs, and shrimp. When you come to the mouth of St. Charles Bay, turn right and follow the pilings south between two small Islands with shell beaches. Paddle east along the marshy shoreline of the Blackjack Peninsula to birdwatch before returning the way you came. Beware of damaging your hull on oyster reefs. Also, strong winds from the south may make the Blackjack Peninsula shoreline choppy.

Goose Island State Park to Cedar Bayou

INTERMEDIATE TO ADVANCED

29 to 31 miles depending on route

This is a great overnight route for wildlife watching. It offers a variety of birds, ribbons of oyster reefs, marshes, shell beaches, and the sand dune communities along the Gulf of Mexico. You may see everything from dolphins to alligators in the water and deer to javelina and feral pigs along the shoreline. In addition, there are shipwrecks along the outer coast near your campsite.

Launch from the public boat ramp at Goose Island State Park and paddle a little over a mile east before turning right and following the navigational pilings between two islands south into Aransas Bay. On this paddle stay away from the Blackjack Peninsula shore-

 Goose Island State Park and the Aransas National Wildlife Refuge. Arrows indicate potential routes to and from Cedar Bayou and through St. CharlesBay. Oyster reefs through these bays pose a significant hazard.

▶ *Unidentified sea anemones washed ashore by a recent storm on the outer coast at Cedar Bayou.*

Goose Island State Park and Black Jack Peninsula

BEGINNING TO INTERMEDIATE

3–6 miles

Launch from the public boat ramp at Goose Island State Park and follow the navigational pilings east a little more than a mile. On your right you may see a series of exposed oyster reefs, depending on the tide. If you paddle over toward one of the reefs, you may carefully pull up a clump of oysters to inspect.

line to save time by staying out of the shallows. After paddling east for a mile or so, you will see the point of Dunham Island in the distance. Stay about 0.3 mile off the southern point of Dunham Island. Paddle across the intracoastal waterway between Poverty and Pelican reef and look for large navigational pilings trailing off to the northeast. Turn northeast and follow the pilings into San Carlos Bay for a little more than a mile. You will see a small island along the right side of the channel. The dredged channel here is called the Cape Carlos Dugout. If there are no birds, the shell bar on the south side of the island provides paddlers with a nice rest stop. From here you may see a myriad of exposed oyster reefs at low tide all over San Carlos Bay. If the tide is high, it looks as if you could paddle across the bay directly to Ballou Island, but don't do it. You will discover very shallow water and lots of oysters that can damage hulls and cut right through rubber soles, should you have to portage over a reef. Be careful! Paddling in such shallow water is difficult and slow, and you must reach your destination or return to Goose Island State Park before dark. For those new to the area, a GPS unit is indispensable.

From the small island, continue northeast along the line of pilings for a little over 2 miles. You will notice you are getting close to Cedar Point on your left. If the tide is not too high, you will see an exposed oyster reef crest (Cedar Reef) to your right. The channel here is called Cedar Dugout and is right off the eastern side of Cedar Point. On your right is a break in the reef just before another small island. Here you can paddle inside Cedar Reef and southeast along the Third Chain of Islands. There is usually a large reddish houseboat moored along the shell beach on the south side of this chain. Paddle a little beyond this to find the small cut (15 feet wide but always passable) between the chain and the northwest tip of Ballou Island, taking you into Mesquite Bay. The shell beach here is an excellent place to rest for a few minutes before heading to Cedar Bayou. From here, paddle about 4 miles southeast to the opening of Cedar Bayou. If you are less adventurous, continue into Mesquite Bay from Cedar Point and then turn southeast for a 4.5- to 5-mile open water crossing of Mesquite Bay. Good landmarks when

▲ *This sailboat was wrecked shortly before I visited Cedar Bayou in 2003; the sails were still intact when I first saw it. But the sea takes its toll. The boat was hardly recognizable by December 2005.*

◄ *A fine specimen of the bivalve* Dosina discus *in the sand at Cedar Bayou. The streaks apparent in the sand matched the prevailing wind direction of a recent storm.*

▶ *Camping at Cedar Bayou as storm clouds move in.*

▶▶ *The shell beach lining the shore of Ballou Island and looking toward Cedar Reef and the Third Chain of Islands.*

crossing Mesquite Bay are the large boathouse on the east side of the bay and Liberty Airport on Matagorda Island. Stay to the right of these landmarks to find the entrance to Cedar Bayou.

Paddle south along Cedar Bayou about 3.5 to 4 miles southwest to reach the dunes where you can camp. At lower tides it may be difficult to reach the camp. When I last visited the area after Hurricane Rita in December of 2005, Cedar Bayou was navigable by kayak all the way into the Gulf of Mexico. This small natural pass is periodically opened by dredging or storms. There is currently a movement to dredge the pass to keep it open all year. For now, the area is accessible only by kayaks or shallow draft power boats. As you paddle down the channel, generally stay to your right. Feel the bottom with your paddle tips to stay in the channel. As you approach the end of the channel there are shallow sand bars with a great number of birds. You have to paddle far to the right of the last bar and then cut left to reach the camping area. Along the foredunes on the north side of the channel

are some signs and half-buried picnic tables marking the area designated for camping.

The dunes along the Gulf provide wonderful beach-combing for seashells. You may find a great number of pen shells and sand dollars washed up here. Sand dollar and pen shell beds form prominent subtidal communities along much of the Texas coast. You will see many of the clams and snails that live in these offshore communities washed up here, because few people visit this beach. Along with shells you will often find the bright orange strands of the common gorgonian called the sea whip. If the tide is low, walk along the beach and you may see mole crabs and coquina clams burrowing in the sand. The distinct small burrow holes in the lower intertidal zone are the work of ghost shrimp; some of their burrows are more than 3 feet deep. Higher up you will see the prominent burrows of ghost crabs, which can be found far into the dunes. Among the many other animals often washed up along the shore are blue and portunid crabs, a variety of starfish, jellyfish, and animals associated with pelagic gulfweed

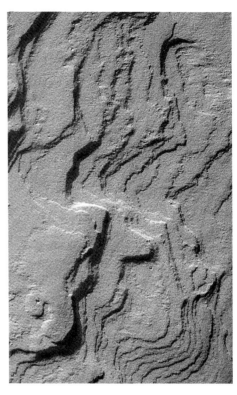

(genus *Sargassum*) that sometimes washes in. The sand bars along the end of Cedar Bayou are often teeming with birds. Occasionally I have seen coyotes trying to hunt these birds early in the morning. In the surrounding shallows I have also seen American eels. If you get up early, you will almost always see deer, rabbits, and coyotes behind the foredunes. If you leave food out, you may also come into contact with large feral pigs.

Looking south along the shoreline, you will see the wreck of the fishing trawler *God's Gift* about 2 miles away. In 2003 a 25- to 30-foot sailboat had just wrecked along the shore, but by December of 2005 this small wreck was almost gone. A good deal of miscellaneous flotsam and jetsam washes ashore. Some artifacts come from oil and gas platforms, but you will notice many of the labels on objects washed ashore are foreign.

After camping overnight, return to Goose Island State Park along the same route. If you are paddling into San Antonio Bay to Hopper's Landing, see the following route.

▲ *Details of how hurricane Rita stripped the foredunes to reveal interesting patterns and formations.*

◀ *The Hurricane Rita storm surge opened Cedar Bayou to the Gulf of Mexico for a short time. Since the advent of the intracoastal waterway and deep passes used for commercial shipping, many natural passes, including Cedar Bayou, have closed. This picture was taken three months after the storm.*

Goose Island State Park to Hopper's Landing

INTERMEDIATE TO ADVANCED

37–38 miles

This route offers a variety of paddling conditions and more scenery and wildlife than any other route on the Texas coast. The best way to paddle this route during prevailing southeasterly winds is from Goose Island State Park to Hopper's Landing, but the route should be reversed if prevailing winds are from the north. Be prepared for long open water crossings and occasionally rough bay waters.

Besides the wildlife and scenery described for the preceding route, there are sand dune bluffs and cliffs along San Antonio Bay with well-developed mottes sculpted by prevailing winds. These sands are part of the 120,000-year-old Ingleside Barrier, very different from the sands of the barrier islands that formed less than 5,000 years ago. The mottes along the San Antonio Bay shoreline are made up of clusters of red bay, laurel, and live oak trees with an understory of American beautyberry and yaupon, among other species. Yaupon is the most abundant shrub on the refuge. Acorns and fruits from these common plants provide an abundance of food for insects, birds, and mammals.

Ghost crabs are conspicuous residents of outer coast dune communities, and larger specimens may have burrows as much as a mile from shore.

For example, live oak acorns make up more than 50 percent of the white-tailed deer population's annual food consumption.

To begin this trip, follow the preceding route from Goose Island State Park to the Cedar Bayou camping area. The second day's paddle is more than 22.5 miles, and there are places where you can get lost, so have a GPS handy and start early. Paddle back north along the bayou 3.5–4 miles. If it is early morning, keep an eye out for deer, pigs, and coyotes along the Matagorda Island shoreline. Paddle 3.5 miles north directly across Mesquite Bay. For the first 1.5 miles there are navigational pilings you can follow due north. From there you should see the small islands to the north, but they may not be distinguishable from the Matagorda Island shoreline. Paddle to the left of these islands to find Ayres Dugout immediately adjacent. Ayres Reef extends northwest from the dugout and is often visible even at high tides. Fishing cabins on these small islands make a good landmark. Once you have paddled through the channel between the oyster reef and the island, then paddle nearly due north again along the Second Chain of Islands for more than 2 miles. You may see boat traffic along the Gulf Intracoastal Waterway ahead and Rattlesnake Island to your left. Paddle along the eastern shore of the islands and look for intracoastal waterway marker #51 as you paddle northeast.

About 3 miles down the waterway, stay out of McMullen Lake while whooping cranes are on the refuge (check with park personnel). Be careful when rounding the point into San Antonio Bay as the water is occasionally rough here. To the northeast is the bird observation tower that overlooks McMullen Lake. You may also see tourists walking along the shoreline trail. It may eventually be possible to land here and visit the observation tower; check with park personnel when you plan your trip. From here northeast along the shoreline, you should see the exposed sand dune cliff at Dagger Point, where a wooden stairway comes down to the beach. It may become possible in the future to land here to rest; again, check with park personnel. If so, climb the stairs and walk the trail through the stunted oaks and red bay trees of a classic motte. This is one of the best and most accessible examples on the coast.

To continue to Hopper's Landing, paddle northeast from Dagger Point parallel to Dagger Point Reef. Although only 20–30 feet wide, the jagged reef crest forms a ribbon of oyster shells extending nearly a mile to the northeast and visible except at higher tides. You will notice two small gas or oil platforms ahead as you follow the reef. The larger of the two is almost straight ahead, and a smaller one is closer inshore on the left. After paddling less than a mile from Dagger Point to the larger platform, turn directly north for about 3.5 miles, staying offshore and out of the shallows until you see Hopper's Landing. Land on the sand and shell beach just south of the small breakwater and store.

St. Charles Bay

INTERMEDIATE

up to 24 miles

If you launch from the public boat ramp on St. Charles Bay just a few hundred feet from the Big Tree, it is about 11.5 miles to the north end of the bay. Just beyond the dam is Burgentine Lake. McAlister and McAlister report that the lake was named for a Spanish brigantine that was washed through St. Charles Bay during a storm. According to local lore, when the storm waters receded the vessel was 6 miles inland on the open prairie. This is a quiet place, with the exception of air boats. Whooping cranes may be viewed occasionally along the eastern shoreline. Alligators are most commonly seen along the northwestern shoreline. If you decide to paddle into a marshy inlet off the main bay, it is good to have a GPS unit. ▮

Beach plants such as beach tea (Croton punctatus) serve as an important food source for many animals and insects.

Aransas Bay and Vicinity

THIS AREA IS ONE OF THE BEST PADDLING destinations on the coast. It is not as isolated as the south coast but is ideal for wildlife watching, fishing, surfing, and watching shipping traffic going to and from the busy port of Corpus Christi. The bays along the central coast are deeper with more stable salinity than those to the north and south. This area is subtropical, with a mixture of temperate and tropical species of algae, invertebrates, and fish. Aransas Pass and adjacent channels serve as the major link to transport larval and adult fish and invertebrates between the bays and the Gulf of Mexico. In the 1950s the famous marine scientist Joel Hedgpeth estimated that the pass was the primary link between the Gulf of Mexico and approximately half a million acres (200,000 hectares) of wetlands. A study in the 1960s estimated that the average biomass passing through Aransas Pass was approximately 700,000 pounds (318,960 kg) per day. In a 1995 study I published in the *Journal of the Marine Biological Association of the United Kingdom,* I documented more than sixty-four species of algae and invertebrates living in the Aransas Pass mid-littoral zone alone. The rich wetland flora, sea grass, algae, and invertebrates of the pass and adjacent bays support large numbers of fish and birds. Birdwatching is a popular pastime for many paddlers, and there are many good guides available, but

Like many birds that live along the shore, the roseate spoonbill (Ajaia ajaja) *has a specialized bill, in this case adapted for moving from side to side in the shallows to strain out small fish, crabs, and shrimp. Photo by Winifred Shrum*

my favorite for this area is *Aransas: A Naturalist's Guide* by Wayne and Martha McAlister. Fishing in this area is also excellent, and several guide services cater to kayakers who fish. Dolphins in a large resident pod are easily observed by paddlers and in fact often approach kayakers. Included in this section is a trip down the Aransas River to Copano Bay, where large animals such as alligators, javelina, feral hogs, and white-tailed deer can often be viewed. Local paddler Ken Johnson describes this trip as the Texas paddler's version of the film *Out of Africa*.

Live Oak Peninsula separates Aransas Bay from Copano Bay. The peninsula's resort towns of Fulton and Rockport provide access to Aransas Bay and offer lodging adjacent to bayside beaches convenient for paddlers traveling north and south. These towns were initially involved in cattle ranching. There were numerous slaughter houses and meat packing plants in the latter half of the nineteenth century. Fulton is named after George Fulton Sr., a local cattle baron who built a large Victorian mansion now maintained by the state. In the late 1800s boatbuilding and fishing began to develop as aspects of the local economy. Shrimping became important in the area in the 1930s. Rockport is now home to the Texas Maritime Museum and largely caters to tourists and fishermen. In addition Rockport Beach Park was designated the first "Blue Wave Beach" in the state of Texas, a designation that certifies the nation's cleanest beaches. Rockport is a great place for kayakers to watch

birds in the quiet waters of Little Bay, to play in gentle surf in Aransas Bay, or to paddle past the beautiful waterfront homes of Key Allegro.

Where the Aransas River widens to meet Copano Bay, Karankawa and Copano Indians congregated at a large oyster reef at Black Point. The Spanish originally used Black Point as a landing that later became a small settlement. In the 1800s Black Point suffered a series of Indian raids and was a supply point for ranchers and the Mexican Army. A mile or two northeast of Black Point was the town of St. Mary's of Aransas on Copano Bay. It was also an important port in the 1800s, used to ship cargo to and from San Antonio, Beeville, Refugio, and Goliad. St. Mary's was destroyed during the Civil War and was finally abandoned after severe storms in the 1880s. Both places are now a part of the town of Bayside. Paddlers can imagine what it might have been like in the old days for Indians and early settlers as they paddle down the Aransas River to watch alligators, javelinas, and other wildlife before passing over the oyster reefs to land on the sandy beaches of Black Point.

The founders of the town of Aransas Pass had intentions of making it a deepwater port, and initial efforts centered around dredging the channel at Port Aransas and building jetties flanking it to access the Gulf of Mexico. Severe hurricanes in 1916 and 1919 devastated and flooded towns in the area, making it clear that the high bluffs and protected shoreline of Corpus Christi would make a much safer port. Since then Aransas Pass

◄ *The bays surrounding Aransas Pass are excellent places to fish for redfish (Sciaenops ocellatus). Photo by Ken Johnson*

▼ *A curious dolphin passing by a paddler on the shoreline. Photo by Ken Johnson*

has primarily remained home to a large fleet of fishing and shrimp boats. Paddlers can take the Ransom Island route to explore the waters adjacent to Aransas Pass.

The pass itself is the deepwater channel that separates San Jose Island on the north from Mustang Island on the south and allows shipping access to Corpus Christi Bay. The original natural pass shifted south over the years, and plans to deepen and stabilize the pass began in the 1880s. However, substantial jetties that stabilized the pass were not completed until about 1919. The Lydia Ann Lighthouse marks the position of the old pass about 1 mile north of its present location. The octagonal red brick lighthouse, the second oldest surviving on the Texas coast, was originally constructed in 1857 and was nearly destroyed during the Civil War. The weathered wooden buildings with wide verandas adjacent to the lighthouse were built in 1917 after a severe hurricane. The lighthouse was closed in 1952, in part because of high maintenance costs. A new light was constructed and is maintained at the Port Aransas Coast Guard Station to better mark the pass. After Hurricane Celia severely damaged the old lighthouse in 1970, prominent Texan Charles Butt restored it and refitted it with an antique Fresnel lens. In July of 1988 the light was recommissioned, and today the fixed white light is visible

Roseate spoonbills flying.
Photo by Winifred Shrum

for about ten miles. Paddlers interested in birdwatching and fishing can explore the black mangrove estuary behind it, on the appropriately named Lighthouse Lakes Paddling Trail.

Port Aransas is the town on the south side of the pass on the northern tip of Mustang Island. The name Aransas is derived from the Aransas Indians who inhabited the area until approximately A.D. 1200. Artifacts from Copano Bay date back four thousand years. Interestingly, the Karankawa Indians arrived not much more than a hundred years before the first Spaniards. Early European settlers used the area for cattle and sheep grazing. The first store was built around 1880 and the first post office opened in 1888, when the town was called Ropesville. In 1896 it was renamed Tarpon for the abundant game fish around the natural pass. The town adopted the name Port Aransas in 1910 or 1911. Paddlers launching from Port Aransas should be careful when crossing the pass as oil tankers and cargo ships may be closer than they appear and moving faster than you realize. Along the beach is I. B. Magee Beach Park, a popular county park where paddlers can camp and surf. The neighboring University of Texas Marine Science Institute is located within walking distance, right on the pass. It has an excellent library and small aquarium well worth visiting, especially if you are unfamiliar with the area's wildlife. Across the channel is San Jose Island, a popular destination for primitive camping and surfing on the outer coast. At one time San Jose Island had a gun turret and military outpost to guard the pass.

Recommended Navigational Aids
Upper Laguna Madre to San Antonio Bay by Hook-N-Line Map Company; *Upper Laguna Madre* by Pasadena Hotspot; *Lighthouse Lakes Paddling Trails Aerial Photocard* or *Photomap* by Shoreline Publishing; aerial maps downloaded from TerraServer (www.terraserver.com), Google Earth (http://earth.google.com), or MapQuest (www.mapquest.com).

Planning Considerations
If you are taking the ferry between Aransas Pass and Port Aransas, be aware that on busy weekends it may take several hours of waiting in line to cross. During

these times it is wise to cross early in the morning or late at night. If you cannot avoid peak hours, it may be wise to drive around the bay and avoid the ferry altogether. If you are paddling into the Lighthouse Lakes trail area, Brown and Root Flats, or Ransom Island Flats, then know when low tides are scheduled and avoid paddling them at these times. Also realize that high winds can affect water levels in this shallow bay system. Low tides, both predicted and those created by strong winds, can strand kayakers on shallow shorelines. Note also that the tidal action in and out of Aransas Pass can be strong. If while crossing the inlet you find you are quickly being moved in or out of the pass, remember to paddle as close to the jetty as possible, as there is often a slight eddy effect or even a countercurrent that will allow you to paddle better against the current.

Only the most experienced paddlers should attempt paddling on the open coast depending on wind and wave action. When trying to make a beach landing on the outer coast during southeast winds, remember there is often diminished wave action just north of Aransas Pass in the lee of the north jetty. An option when camping on the outer coast on San Jose Island across the pass from Port Aransas is for friends or family to join paddlers by taking the Jetty Boat from Fisherman's Wharf in Port Aransas across the channel to San Jose Island (361-749-5448). A cell phone is usually adequate for emergencies. Be prepared to call the Port Aransas Coast Guard Station for emergencies at 361-749-5217.

Accommodations

In Port Aransas, Nueces County's I. B. Magee Beach Park is located just south of the jetty along the beach facing the Gulf of Mexico. Primitive camping, RV sites, a laundry, picnic tables, and showering facilities are available (361-749-6117). Accommodations in this area are too numerous to list, but contact the Chamber of Commerce for Port Aransas (361-749-5919, www.portaransas.org), Aransas Pass (www.aransaspass.org), and Rockport/Fulton (361-729-6445, www.rockport-fulton.org). For paddlers passing through Aransas Bay or those who want direct access to the water, the Sand Dollar Resort Motel and RV Park (877-463-4747) is a good choice close to a launch point.

Directions to Launch Sites

Fulton: North of Rockport in Fulton, east of Highway 35, is North Fulton Beach Road along Aransas Bay, where you can park and launch from the sandy shoreline. The Sand Dollar Resort Motel and RV Park (877-463-4747), located between Highway 35 and Fulton Beach Road, is a convenient place for kayakers to stay when paddling north or south along Aransas Bay, with the Sand Dollar Marina and a restaurant on the water. Kayakers can launch and land from the adjacent beach right across from the motel. Boats can be kept at the motel.

Rockport Beach Park: North of Aransas Pass in Rockport, kayakers can access Aransas Bay and the Key Allegro area from Rockport Beach Park (361-727-2158 or

◄ *A portunid swimming crab* (Arenaeus cribrarius), *found along the shore at Port Aransas.*

▼ *The American white pelican* (Pelecanus erythrorhynchos) *uses its large, specialized bill to catch fish. Photo by Winifred Shrum*

877-929-7977). Turn at the sign for the beach park directly off of Highway 35 just south of Little Bay. There are showers, restrooms, and picnic areas. Drive to the end of the road in the park, where you can launch in the small sailboat area. More experienced paddlers can launch from the main beach.

Aransas River: Just south of Bayside, Black Point is on the north side of the FM 136. The bridge crosses the mouth of the Aransas River at the east end of Copano Bay. On the northeast side of the FM 136 bridge there are sandy shores adjacent to an old TPWD boat ramp that is a suitable landing site on Black Point after paddling down the Aransas River. Drive a little over 4 miles north of Bayside on FM 136 and turn left on FM 1360. Drive approximately 6.5 miles west and turn south on CR 629. Paddlers can park and launch at the TPWD boat ramp about 1.5 miles south at the end of the road on the Aransas River. After paddling down the river, cross under the FM 136 bridge and land on the beach at Black Point as described.

Ransom Island: In Aransas Pass travel south on Commercial Street (also Highway 361) to Ransom Avenue. Turn east on Ransom Avenue across the railroad tracks, where the road turns into East Ransom Road. At the end of the road is Ransom Park, where there are a public boat ramp for launching, restrooms, and nicely shaded picnic shelters.

Harbor Island/Lighthouse Lakes: The Harbor Island Loop or Lighthouse Lakes trails can be accessed off Highway 361 between Aransas Pass and Port Aransas. One of the easiest places to launch is from the Fin and Feather Marina less than 2 miles east of Aransas Pass, on the east end of Stedman Island off Highway 361. Many people also launch from Highway 361 a mile or two farther southeast, where the highway parallels Aransas Channel. This area is now called the Lighthouse Lakes Trails Park. Many people launch from a local landmark called the Crab Man Marina.

Port Aransas: At Robert's Point Park east of the ferry landing you can launch from the public boat ramp into the Port Aransas boat harbor. There are picnic facilities and restrooms at the park. If there is no parking, there is an old unused boat ramp on the west side of Woody's Sport's Center on the south side of the harbor on Cotter Avenue. If you choose the latter, make sure you obtain permission from the staff at Woody's. Those experienced with surf can launch from the beach adjacent to the south jetty in I. B. Magee Beach Park. Restrooms and outdoor showers are available to the public on the beach. Those who pay to camp at I. B. Magee Beach Park have access to much nicer restroom and showering facilities.

A laughing gull (Larus atricilla), in breeding plumage. Photo by Carmen Hagopian

Side Trips

The Fulton Mansion (361-729-0386, www.visitfultonmansion.com) and Texas Maritime Museum in the Rockport area are well worth visiting (361-729-6644, www.texasmaritimemuseum.org). The Aquarium at Rockport Harbor is also interesting (361-729-2328, www.rockportaquarium.com). The small aquarium and museum at the University of Texas Marine Science Institute in Port Aransas are worth seeing also (361-749-6729, www.utmsi.utexas.edu/visit).

Fulton to Goose Island State Park

INTERMEDIATE TO ADVANCED

5–5.75 miles

Paddle along the shoreline north from the Sand Dollar Resort Motel and then veer northeast toward Goose Island. As you approach, you will see the long pier that extends from the east side of Goose Island. Watch for oyster reefs as you approach and paddle into the mouth of St. Charles Bay to the east of the island before turning west to follow the pilings behind Goose Island to the boat ramp. This is a good choice if it is rough or if you are paddling one way to be picked up from Goose Island. If it is very rough, follow the navigational pilings east of the island and on the east side of the mouth of St. Charles Bay. You will then come to additional pilings that mark the route west to the boat ramp behind Goose Island. Alternatively, if you plan to camp on Goose Island, approach the front of the island, where there are picnic shelters associated with these bayfront camp sites. These are often the best camp sites because the prevailing wind helps control the mosquitoes.

Rockport Beach Park

BEGINNING TO ADVANCED

1–5 miles

This clean little beach park is a great place for all skill levels. Rockport Beach was the first certified "Blue Wave Beach" in the state of Texas, a designation signifying that the beach is clean and well maintained and the water quality is good for swimming. There are restroom facilities, showers, and picnic shelters. More experienced kayakers can launch from the outer beach, while inexperienced paddlers should launch in the boat channel in the area designated as the "small sailboat launch area," just down from the saltwater swimming lagoon. The main beach can get significant surf from prevailing southeast winds but is a great area for more experienced paddlers to play. Those less experienced or interested in birdwatching and paddling through Key Allegro to see the beautiful homes can launch in the boat channel adjacent to Little Bay. If you are paddling one way from Port Aransas, then this is a great place to land to end the trip.

◄ *Rockport Beach Park.*

▼ *Aransas River to Copano Bay.*

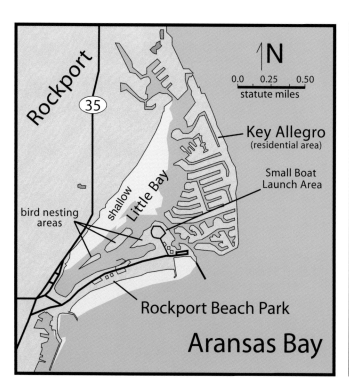

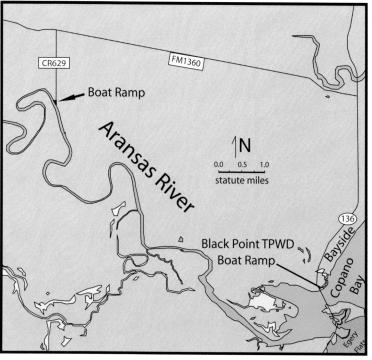

▲ *The black skimmer (Rynchops niger) uses its dagger-shaped bill with longer lower mandible to impale fish as it "skims" over the water. Photo by Winifred Shrum*

▶ *American alligators are a common sight along the Aransas River and are not dangerous unless provoked. Photo by Ken Johnson*

▶▶ *A quiet paddle down the serene Aransas River. Photo by Ken Johnson*

Aransas River to Copano Bay's Black Point

BEGINNER TO INTERMEDIATE

11–11.5 miles

This trip is very interesting. The flora begins with huge stands of reeds (9–12 feet high) and millet, which progress to smaller more salt-tolerant plants as you approach Copano Bay. There are large numbers of alligators here and there may be feral pigs and javelina as well. The birdwatching along the river is amazing. It begins at the TPWD boat ramp at the end of CR 629. Follow the river about 2 miles down and you will begin to see alligators or their nests, as they have knocked down vegetation where they exit the water. Beware of floating logs that may turn out to be alligators. The animals are not dangerous unless provoked or approached too closely. Respect is the key word. About 10 miles down is a large mud flat to the left and crab traps are scattered about. You may see fiddler crabs along the shore here, and oysters are a threat at low tide. Stay to the right of the inlet before heading toward the Highway 136 bridge. Cross under the north end of the bridge to land on the sandy beach at Black Point on the east side.

Ransom Island Loop

BEGINNING TO INTERMEDIATE

8.5–9.0 miles

Ransom Park in Aransas Pass has restroom facilities, nicely shaded picnic tables, and grills for large groups. From the public boat ramp paddle southeast along Ransom Channel to cross the intracoastal waterway past markers #42 and #41. Continue southeast about 1.5 miles around Ransom Island. Paddle south less than a mile to reach East Dagger Island. Paddle along its eastern shoreline and then turn west for about 1.3 miles. Look for the pilings that mark the United Pipeline Channel. Follow the channel northwest to the intracoastal waterway. Paddle northeast along the intracoastal past the shipyards. Turn northwest at intracoastal waterway markers #41 and #42 and follow the channel back to the public boat ramp at Ransom Park. Many people fish the grass flats north of Ransom Island and on the west side of Ransom Island when the tide is high.

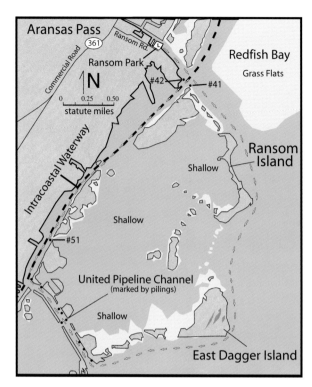

Ransom Island Loop. L *indicates launch site.*

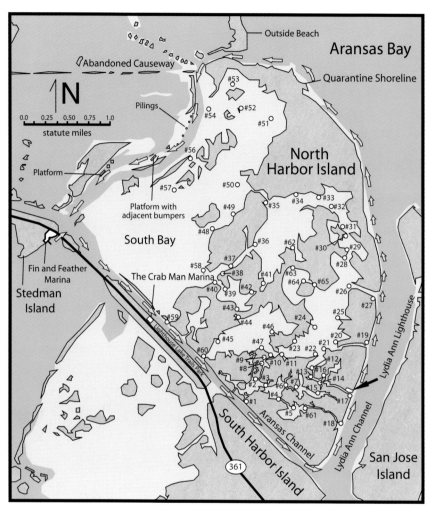

Harbor Island Loop or Lighthouse Lakes Paddling Trails

BEGINNING TO INTERMEDIATE

up to 15 miles

Depending on the wind, tides and your goals, there are two approaches to paddling North Harbor Island and the Lighthouse Lakes trails. You can circumnavigate North Harbor Island or you can explore the interior of the island via the Lighthouse Lakes trails. The circumnavigation of North Harbor Island is less than 13.5 miles and can be paddled almost without regard to tidal height. If water levels permit, an optional detour to observe part of the black mangrove estuary in the island's interior extends the route to approximately 15 miles. The best place to start this trip is at the Fin and Feather Marina less than 2 miles east of Aransas Pass, on the east end of Stedman Island off Highway 361. Since the prevailing winds out of the southeast are usually weaker early in the morning, starting from the

northwest means you do not have to paddle directly into the wind later in the day. From the boat ramp paddle under the Highway 361 bridge and down the Aransas Channel parallel to the highway. The open expanse of water to the left is South Bay. About 1.5 miles from the ramp, you will pass the Crab Man Marina on your right. Continue down the channel on the left side for about 2.5 miles and turn left into the Lydia Ann Channel. As you follow the shoreline around there is a nice beach where you can stop to rest and watch the ship traffic. You may also see the *MV Texas Treasure,* a large cruise ship used to take passengers offshore to gamble. Dolphins are commonly seen here. More experienced paddlers who are hungry, thirsty, or need

Lighthouse Lakes and the Lydia Ann Lighthouse. Numbered GPS markers have been placed to help guide kayakers along the Lighthouse Lakes Paddling Trails but should not be relied on because they may be missing and marker map locations may not match actual locations precisely.

The black mangrove (Avicennia germinans) forms dense "mangals" abundant along the Lighthouse Lakes Paddling Trail on Harbor Island. Photo by Ken Johnson

Fishing along the sea grass flats and channels may reward anglers with speckled sea trout, redfish, or flounder. Paddle back out of the inlet and continue north along the Lydia Ann Channel into Aransas Bay along what is called the Quarantine Shoreline, where nice sand and shell beaches provide a good spot to rest or eat lunch. If you walk quietly along the beach and look into the estuary, you may see some interesting birds. From here paddle west into the inlet between Harbor Island and Outside Beach (marked on some maps as Corpus Christi Bayou). Follow the shoreline of Harbor Island around into the channel that goes generally southwest. You will see some pilings that mark the channel and then a small oil platform along the back of a small island. Paddle past this and you will see three other small oil platforms to the southwest. When you reach these, you should see the Highway 361 bridge at the Fin and Feather Marina where you began.

supplies can cross the channel and enter Port Aransas Harbor adjacent to Robert's Point Park. Otherwise continue north along the Lydia Ann Channel less than a mile to reach the Lydia Ann Lighthouse (described in the introduction to this section). Since the lighthouse is privately owned and there are people living there, please respect their privacy by not landing.

After passing the lighthouse, you will notice extensive stands of marsh grasses along the channel. You may see large marsh periwinkles migrating up and down the stems with the tide. At low tides farther along the shore you may encounter thousands of fiddler crabs, the males waving their oversized chelipeds as they skitter down the shoreline to escape into their burrows. Over a mile north of the lighthouse is a large inlet into the Lighthouse Lakes. Paddling into the mangrove estuary and sea grass flats to look around, birdwatch, or fish, adds a mile or two to the 13.5-mile circumnavigation of North Harbor Island. If you paddle into the inlet, then you may see GPS marker #26 for the Redfish Loop of the Lighthouse Lakes Paddling Trail (discussed later). The black mangroves found here do not attain the status of trees but are merely shrubs less than 3 feet high; they get much larger in South Texas.

To investigate the Lighthouse Lakes Paddling Trail, you will need either the aerial photocard or photomap and a GPS unit to navigate accurately. Although I have been told that TPWD maintains and replaces all the GPS markers, damage from weather and vandalism does occur. To access the area, drive past the Fin and Feather Marina (see preceding route) and cross the Highway 361 causeway east from Stedman Island to reach Lighthouse Lakes Trails Park. Launch just past the Crab Man Marina to access the starting point for the South Bay Loop at GPS marker #59 (see map). This loop is about 6.7 miles. Launch about 0.75 mile past the Crab Man to access Cutter's Loop, where you will see marker #60 just inside the small inlet. The loop is approximately 5 miles long. To access the Redfish Loop, park along the shore to the southeast just before the next bridge. From here you can paddle approximately 0.3–0.4 mile southeast along the Aransas Channel to the inlet where you see marker #1 to begin the loop. The loop is 6.8 miles long and can be extended to about 9 miles if you add on the Electric Lake Loop. On the way back, it is faster to paddle back by marker #44 to marker #60, where Cutter's Loop begins and ends, and then return southeast along the Aransas Channel to your starting point.

Port Aransas/Lydia Ann Lighthouse Loop

INTERMEDIATE TO ADVANCED

9.5+ miles

This is one of my favorite routes. It includes barrier island dunes, jetties flanking a typical Texas pass with large ships coming and going, and bayside marshes and mangroves around an old lighthouse. Launch from Robert's Point Park and paddle out of the small harbor at Port Aransas with care to avoid boat traffic. Once outside the breakwater, paddle east along the shoreline of Port Aransas. The last pier and group of buildings in the channel belong to the University of Texas Marine Science Institute, and the small boat marina before you reach the pier is used by the school. You may see the local pilot boat (bright orange) used to guide ships in and out of the pass here. You can stop at the boat ramp in the small marina or at one of the small beaches along the channel to walk the campus and visit the school's small aquarium to learn more about the marine life in the area. The campus also has an interpretive trail open to the public.

Check for boat traffic before crossing the pass to the north jetty that flanks San Jose Island. You may see the small pier used by the Jetty Boat from Port Aransas to transport people to San Jose Island. Be prepared to see dolphins in the channel. Members of a resident pod often congregate in the sandy shallows adjacent to the north jetty, which has less boating traffic and fewer people. If the weather is calm and the tide is low, you might paddle close to the jetty to look at the marine life in the intertidal zone. Cabbage head jellyfish are often seen floating in the pass. Wave action increases noticeably as you paddle toward the end of the jetty. If you are not experienced with paddling in the surf, turn around at this point. On the other hand, if you are, then continue out and around the jetty.

If the tide is going out, there are often steeper breaking waves at the end of the jetty. Be careful to stay well clear of the rocks at the end of the jetty and take a few minutes to watch for wave sets. As you paddle toward shore look for a fence line to the north on San Jose Island. The island is privately owned, and visitors should not land or camp north of this bound-

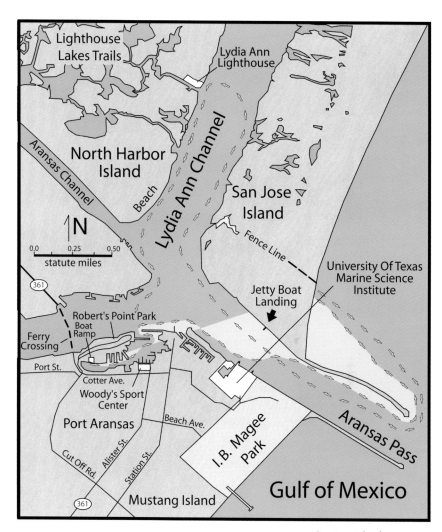

ary. As all visitors to the island with the exception of kayakers have to carry their gear from the pier in the channel, I prefer to camp near the fence line, as it is more secluded.

It is about a 3.5-mile trip from Robert's Point Park to the beach on San Jose Island. From late spring to early fall the foredunes are often carpeted with morning glories and other flowers in bloom. Strong onshore winds blowing off the water help cool things down in the summer. I suspect the large flocks of birds often congregate along this shoreline during the summer months for this reason and because there are few or no vehicles driving down the beach to disturb them. Many times I paddle further down the shore just to

San Jose Island, Port Aransas, and the Lydia Ann Lighthouse. Only experienced paddlers should venture outside Aransas Pass into the Gulf of Mexico.

The Lydia Ann Lighthouse near Port Aransas was originally constructed in 1857 and was named after the daughter of lighthouse keeper Frank Stevenson, who was appointed in 1897. Photo by Ken Johnson

birdwatch and surf. As you walk along the beach you may notice large numbers of ghost crab holes not commonly seen in places where people routinely drive on the beach. Although largely nocturnal, these fist-sized orange crabs with stalked eyes can be seen in the early morning and late afternoon skittering sideways along the beach. Their burrows get larger as you proceed from the water up the beach and into the dunes. The larger animals live farther from the water. An evening walk watching them can be quite entertaining, but a large crab in your sleeping bag may not be! At certain times of the year, floating clumps of the pelagic brown seaweed *Sargassum*—(actually macroalgae)—wash ashore. If you see a floating tea-colored clump, you might capture it in a plastic container filled with seawater for closer examination. This may reveal a variety of camouflaged animals that inhabit the weed, including small sea anemones, crabs, shrimp, and fish specifically adapted to living in this floating community.

If you camp along the beach near the fence line, you may notice a break in the foredunes. Many years

ago a large storm surge broke through the foredunes and caused considerable erosion. Occasionally fossil shells are revealed in the exposed sediments far behind the foredunes. Walking back toward the jetties well behind the foredunes you may see a large man-made berm, where I have been told there once was a firing range and a cannon that was used to guard the pass during World War II.

If you walk down to the north jetty at low tide, you will see the jumble of 6- to 10-ton blocks of granite and sandstone covered with marine animals and plants. At very low tides you can see that the animals and plants are segregated into approximately three vertical bands (tripartite zonation) formed by a complex gradient of physiological tolerances and biological interactions. The highest band or supralittoral zone is dominated by a semi-terrestrial isopod called a rock roach and small black littorine snails grazing on microalgae. The midlittoral zone is characterized by a variety of different barnacles and the pulmonate limpet (*Siphonaria pectinata*), with a shieldlike shell. Below this is a dense algal turf primarily composed of red or rhodophycean algal turf along with oysters and mussels. In among them are small epiphytic crustaceans, primarily amphipods, and occasionally sea anemones and sea urchins. The most interesting predators in this zone are the stone crab and oyster drill. They both feed on oysters and mussels and on each other: stone crabs can feed on oyster drills, but it has also been shown that large oyster drills can feed on juvenile stone crabs. Of course there are many more animals, including the foot-long sea slug *Aplysia,* which is occasionally seen swimming along the jetties, and at night you may glimpse an octopus, moray eel, or a variety of fishes along the jetties. Fishing around the jetties is usually good all year. If you walk northwest along the channel toward the small pier used by the jetty boat you will usually see dolphins, especially in the evening.

At certain times of the year, often early summer or in August if things have been calm, the warm water clears up enough to go snorkeling. If you walk past the jetty boat pier you may see a few tide pools on the island side of the walkway. Here under some rocks you may find the snapping shrimp *Alpheus* or the porcelain crab *Petrolisthes.* At night or in the early morning, lucky visitors may see coyotes, deer, rabbits, or feral hogs. To learn more about the biology of the coast, I strongly recommend *Shore Ecology of the Gulf of Mexico* by Britton and Morton, available at the bookstore at the University of Texas Marine Science Institute.

After exploring the island or camping, paddle back out and around the jetty into the channel along the north jetty. The large quarry blocks give way to smaller rocks toward the back of the island. Stone crabs are often prolific among the smaller rocks. There is a shallow bar as you round the back of San Jose Island. This is a great area to fish for flounder. Follow the Lydia Ann Channel about a mile north and cross over to see the Lydia Ann Lighthouse. Originally built in 1857, it was named for the daughter of lighthouse keeper Frank Stevenson, who was appointed in 1897 (see section introduction for complete history). The buildings around the lighthouse, constructed in 1917 after a hurricane, are private residences and are off limits to the public. The lighthouse is on Harbor Island, which is surrounded by marsh, and there are small black mangroves or "mangles" in and around the small lakes in the interior. At low tide you may see burrows dotting the shoreline with many fiddler crabs milling about. They are easily recognized as males have a peculiar enlarged claw used to attract mates and defend territory. Adjacent to the lighthouse is a small channel into the interior of Harbor Island. If the tide is high, take a few minutes to explore the island's waterways.

Paddle back south along the Lydia Ann Channel toward the Aransas Channel. As you approach this intersection the shore becomes sandy beach, a great place to take a break before crossing the ship channel to return to the harbor and Robert's Point Park at Port Aransas. Stopping for a rest on the shore allows you to take a few minutes to watch the ship channel, where you may see dolphins playing in the sandy shallows, sizable tankers, intracoastal barges, and the ferry to Port Aransas.

Port Aransas to Rockport or Fulton

INTERMEDIATE TO ADVANCED
18–18.5 miles to Rockport Beach, 21–21.5 miles to the Sand Dollar Resort Motel in Fulton
This route is a great path through Aransas Bay that includes the Lydia Ann Lighthouse, the marshes and mangals of North Harbor Island, shell beaches along the back of San Jose Island, and usually good surfing with prevailing winds into Rockport or Fulton to finish the trip. If winds are from the southeast, then waves increase and require more effort during the last 3.5–6.5 miles of this potentially dangerous open water crossing. People who are not experienced or not very fit should not attempt this. Starting from Robert's Point Park in Port Aransas, carefully paddle across the channel to the back of San Jose Island and follow the Lydia Ann Channel north. Cross the channel about a mile up for a good look at the Lydia Ann Lighthouse. As you paddle north, you may decide to take a brief detour into the marsh for fishing or birdwatching (see preceding route) but not too far, as this is already a long paddle.

Paddle north along North Harbor Island to the Quarantine Shore, a great place for a rest stop. Then

▶ *Ron Duke paddling away from San Jose Island, where we had been camping.*

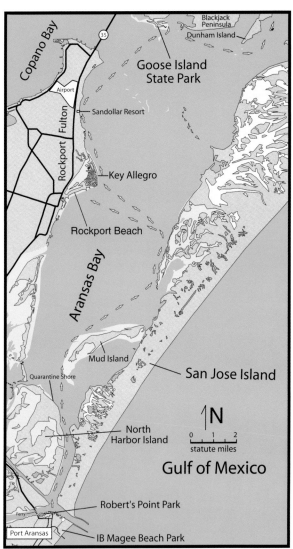

▲ *Port Aransas to Goose Island State Park. Arrows indicate potential routes from Port Aransas to Rockport, Fulton, and Goose Island State Park.*

continue north to make a more than 2-mile open water crossing to round the west end of Mud Island. Follow the shoreline of the island around and make a 3.5-mile open water crossing to reach a strand of shell and sand beaches along the back of San Jose Island. These are great beaches to stop and rest and check the shallow lagoons for birds before the final open water crossing. If the winds are strong out of the southeast and you are not fit and experienced, do not think you can cross even if the water seems calm.

The Rockport water tower and Key Allegro may be the only references for navigation. If they are not in view, they should be the first navigational references to come into view. If you are going to Rockport Beach, paddle northwest to the left of Key Allegro and land in the channel at the "small sailboat launch area" at the park or directly on Rockport Beach (see Rockport

Beach Park map). If you are paddling to Fulton's Sand Dollar Resort Motel, paddle northeast to the right of Key Allegro. Paddle down the shoreline around the restaurant to the small beach across from the motel where paddlers can stay. On a windy day, experienced paddlers will have a great time surfing the wind waves across Aransas Bay. Those staying at the motel have the option to paddle back to Port Aransas or on to Goose Island State Park. If you are headed back to Port Aransas, you might try to get through the small channel on the east side of Mud Island and follow the San Jose Island shoreline if the tide is high. ◼

Corpus Christi Bay

THE SHORELINE ALONG THE city waterfront of Corpus Christi and the eastern shore of the bay offer some interesting paddling. Corpus Christi Bay was named by Diego Ortiz Parrilla, who explored the coast in 1756. What is now Corpus Christi was originally a trading post established in 1839 by Colonel Henry Lawrence Kinney to sell supplies to a Mexican revolutionary army that camped west of Corpus Christi Bay. The city was named after the bay by settlers who moved into the area from the lower Rio Grande Valley in the 1860s. After two hurricanes with significant storm tides devastated the Rockport, Aransas Pass, and Port Aransas areas in 1916 and 1919, it became apparent that the high bluff and protected shoreline at Corpus Christi

The twin towers of the Shoreline Plaza dominate the skyline for paddlers exploring the Corpus Christi waterfront. Photo by Ken Johnson

would be ideal for a deepwater port. Since the town was served by three railroads, the plan was adopted and the port was opened in 1926. Initially the port primarily exported cotton, but in the late 1930s oil replaced cotton as the major export. At one time it was estimated that there were 89 oil fields with more than 3,500 wells within a 125-mile radius of the Port of Corpus Christi. In 1941 Naval Air Station Corpus Christi was commissioned on the south side of Corpus Christi Bay. In 1947 Corn Products Refining Company opened near the port to process sorghum grains into starch, sugar, and syrup. A grain elevator was constructed and opened at the port in 1953. In 1988 Naval Station Ingleside was established on the north side of Corpus Christi Bay. The port was designated a foreign trade zone in 1985 and subsequent efforts have led to successful diversification of cargoes and trade with Mexico, Latin America, Europe, Africa, and Russia. In other words, this is and will continue to be a busy port. Paddling along the waterfront offers spectacular sights, including routine shipping traffic, the shrimp fleet, the aircraft carrier *USS Lexington,* and the gleaming twin towers of Shoreline Plaza built on the city's seawall. There are many beaches where you can paddle up to have a picnic and some where you can eat at an outdoor restaurant and listen to live music.

Beyond describing the Corpus Christi waterfront, I concentrate mainly on the eastern side of Corpus Christi Bay since it is the only portion without industrial or military development. In the post–Civil War years the cattle business boomed in South Texas. Plants called packeries for processing cattle for hides and tallow were built on a natural pass close to Corpus Christi. For this reason the pass was named Packery Pass. It separates Padre Island from Mustang Island, and has been reopened with dredging, and is flanked by two new jetties that extend into the Gulf of Mexico. This pass provides excellent access for paddlers to the Gulf of Mexico, including Bob Hall Pier and Padre Island, which is a few miles south of the pass, and Mustang Island State Park north of the pass. Originally built in 1950, the 300-foot-long Bob Hall Pier was named after a prominent Corpus Christi businessman and veteran of the Spanish-American War. The pier was destroyed by Hurricane Carla in 1961 and again by Hurricane Allen in 1980. The current pier is

1,240 feet long and was completed in 1983. It is thought to be storm proof and was designed with concrete deck squares that pop out when waves strike the underside of the pier to allow the primary framework of the structure to remain. There is a restaurant at the base of the pier and camping along the beach, complete with showering facilities and picnic tables. All of this is within Nueces County's Balli Park, named after Padre Nicolas Balli, the Portuguese Catholic priest for whom Padre Island was named. This park is a great destination for paddlers and a local landmark on the outer Gulf Coast. Those who enjoy camping in solitude can paddle a few more miles south, where primitive camping is allowed.

Mustang Island along the eastern side of the bay was originally called Wild Horse Island in the 1800s by Spaniards, who brought in wild horses called *mesteños.* The area was used extensively for cattle grazing. Mustang Island State Park, established in 1979, provides good access to bayside habitats and camping along the Gulf of Mexico for paddlers. The jetties on the north side of the park are great to surf and fish around. At low tide a variety of intertidal marine life can be seen. Along Corpus Christi Bay to the north of the state park, the Shamrock Island Refuge and the Francine Cohn Preserve were established in 1995 and 2000 respectively and are managed by the Nature Conservancy. Small sandy or shell beaches line the east side of Corpus Christi Bay with shallow channels and wetlands behind. Along the bayside beachfront is a population of black mangrove trees in the preserve. Around these shrubby plants are roots called pneumatophores projecting from the sediment. These "air roots" help supply the plants with oxygen. In the marshy wetlands habitat, smooth cordgrass and glassworts predominate. Along the bayshore and Shamrock Island, a variety of interesting birds are present: migrating and resident songbirds, shorebirds, colonial nesting birds, raptors, and wading birds. Piping plovers, reddish egrets, tricolored herons, peregrine falcons, great blue herons, ibises, roseate spoonbills, and many waterfowl are often seen.

Recommended Navigational Aids
Upper Laguna Madre to San Antonio Bay by Hook-N-Line Map Company; *Wilson's Pass* by Shoreline

Publishing; aerial maps downloaded from TerraServer (www.terraserver.com), Google Earth (http://earth .google.com), or MapQuest (www.mapquest.com).

Planning Considerations

For additional information about kayaking in the Central Texas or Corpus Christi area, contact Ken Johnson (361-855-3926, home.earthlinknet/~johnsonkw/ kayak-corpus/. Good compass skills and/or a GPS unit are useful along the eastern side of Corpus Christi Bay. The aerial photomap produced by Shoreline Publishing gives GPS coordinates that correlate with markers placed at intervals for routes along Fish Pass, Wilson's Pass (or Cut), and Shamrock Island along the eastern shoreline of the bay. Although GPS coordinates may be accurate, paddlers must realize that the positions of markers shown on the aerial map are often different from their position in the field, and some have been removed or vandalized by local residents uninterested in sharing their backyard with visitors. If you find yourself lost in the marsh along any of the eastern bayside routes, then just paddle north or south until you find the first waterway west to reach the sandy bars that line Corpus Christi Bay. For emergencies dial 911 or call the Port Aransas Coast Guard Station at 361-749-5217. For information on conditions in the area call Mustang Island State Park 361-749-5246.

Accommodations

For a stay in the city, the Radisson Hotel or Holiday Inn on Corpus Christi Bay are good choices. For additional information on the city, contact the Corpus Christi Convention and Visitors Bureau at 1201 North Shoreline Boulevard (800-678-6232, www.corpuschristi-tx-cvb.org/). For camping contact Mustang Island State Park (361-749-5246, www.tpwd.state.tx.us/spdest/findadest/parks/mustang island/) or Padre Balli Park (361-949-8121, Nueces County Parks Department, Box 18608, Corpus Christi, TX 78480). Both provide electricity and water with restrooms and showers. Primitive camping is allowed along the outer coast in undeveloped areas.

Directions to Launch Sites

Corpus Christi Waterfront: There are three places commonly used to launch and land to see the Corpus

Inside the Corpus Christi breakwater paddlers can launch and explore the marinas. Photo by Ken Johnson

Christi waterfront: Cooper's Alley L-Head Pier, Emerald Beach, and North Shore. To access Cooper's Alley L-Head Pier and Emerald Beach, take the Morgan Street exit off the Crosstown Expressway. Drive east on Morgan Avenue to South Shoreline Boulevard. Turn north on South Shoreline Boulevard, turn right at the Holiday Inn, and drive around the building to the public lot on the south side. Stairs lead down to Emerald Beach. If going to the L-Head Pier, continue north on South

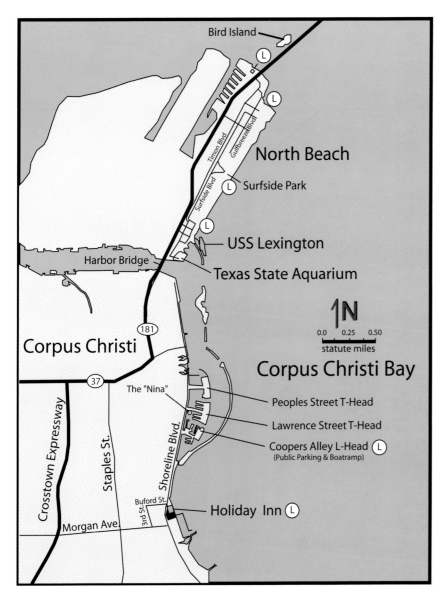

North Beach

Surfside Park

USS Lexington

Texas State Aquarium

Harbor Bridge

Corpus Christi

Corpus Christi Bay

The "Nina"

Peoples Street T-Head

Lawrence Street T-Head

Coopers Alley L-Head
(Public Parking & Boatramp)

Holiday Inn

Bird Island

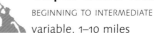

0.0   0.25   0.50
statute miles

Corpus Christi water-
front. L marks the many
places to launch, depend-
ing on conditions and
experience.

island bird refuge (see waterfront route description for details).

Mustang Island State Park: Drive south of Corpus Christi on Highway 358/South Padre Island Drive over the Kennedy Causeway and turn left on Highway 361. Travel north approximately 4.5 miles to get to Mustang Island State Park.

Wilson's Cut: Drive about 4.8 miles north of Mustang Island State Park and turn left. Drive a short distance to a parking area on the south side of the pass and launch from a sandy beach. This parking area is not used as heavily by power boaters. Drive 4.9 miles north of Mustang Island State Park on Highway 361 to reach the road and parking area on the east and north side of Wilson's Cut. Slightly north of the park entrance is a bridge that crosses Fish Pass (now closed to the Gulf). To access Fish Pass, you can park in the dirt lot south of the bridge or take the dirt road on the north side of the pass and park anywhere along the north side of the channel.

Packery Channel Park: Drive south on Highway 358, which becomes South Padre Island Drive over the Kennedy Causeway from Corpus Christi. Look for the visitor's center sign or Packery Channel Park sign immediately after crossing the causeway. Turn left and follow the road back to the channel, where you can park along the shore and launch. This road is the second left after crossing the causeway. Alternatively, if you are going on an overnight trip, you might take the first left, drive under the causeway, and park over by Snoopy's Restaurant. Padre Balli Park and Bob Hall Pier are about 2.5 miles past the visitor center after you cross the Kennedy Causeway.

Shoreline Boulevard and turn right at Cooper's Alley onto the L-Head Pier. Drive out by the bait stand at the end of the pier to access the boat ramp to launch. To get to the North Beach, get off Highway 181 at Beach Avenue. Drive east to Gulfbreeze Avenue and turn left to drive north to Bryan Street and park along the water to launch. For a deeper, more sheltered launch continue on Bryan Street to Hull Street and cross under the Highway 181 causeway bridge to park along the water and launch. The latter provides better access to the small

Corpus Christi Waterfront

BEGINNING TO INTERMEDIATE
variable, 1–10 miles

This shoreline offers wonderful sandy beaches combined with spectacular views of the city and some of its attractions. Sights along the shoreline include the retired aircraft carrier *USS Lexington,* the Texas State Aquarium, and the magnificent twin towers of Shoreline Plaza. The *USS Lexington,* or the "Blue Ghost," served our nation for nearly fifty years and now serves as a floating maritime museum. The Texas State Aquarium is an excellent place to become familiar with marine life along the Texas Gulf Coast. Built on the Corpus Christi seawall, the 411-foot-tall Shoreline Plaza was specially designed to withstand hurricanes and is considered to be one of architect Philip Johnson's major achievements.

The easiest and most sheltered launch is from the public boat ramp at the terminus of the Cooper's Alley L-Head Pier. From the launch to the *Lexington* and back is approximately 3.5 miles and you can paddle primarily in the inner protected harbor. A replica of Christopher Columbus's ship *La Niña* is afloat along the south side of the base of the Lawrence Street T-Head Pier. This ship and two others were donated to Corpus Christi by Spain. However, the other two ships were damaged in an accident with a barge. The damaged vessels can be viewed at the local science museum. Farther north beyond the Shoreline Plaza towers are the new federal courthouse and American Bank Center Sports Complex, cargo docks, the Harbor Bridge, Texas State Aquarium, and a large breakwater with the *Lexington* beyond.

To access Emerald Beach, pull into the Holiday Inn and go around to the right, where there is a public parking area next to the hotel with direct beach access. If you are visiting Corpus Christi, the Holiday Inn is a convenient place to stay because of its access to the water. Launching from here, it is approximately 5 miles north to the *Lexington* and back. Some of the islands that form part of the breakwater system serve as bird rookeries during the spring and are off limits during that time. Remember, if the wind increases from the south, it can make for a long paddle back to the launch, and it might be a good idea to loop into the inner harbor for part of the return trip. Also, you can paddle south along the shore for a few miles to enjoy the beautiful homes and mansions of the Corpus Christi waterfront.

Along the north shore there are many options, but the best is to drive under the Highway 181 Causeway from North Beach on Hull Street (see Directions to Launch Sites) and park along the water. From here it is less than a quarter of a mile to reach the small island

◀ *A replica of Christopher Columbus's ship* La Niña *can be seen at the base of the Lawrence Street T-head pier. Photo by Ken Johnson*

▼ *A kayaker is dwarfed by the* USS Lexington *as he paddles around the monolithic aircraft carrier. Photo by Ken Johnson*

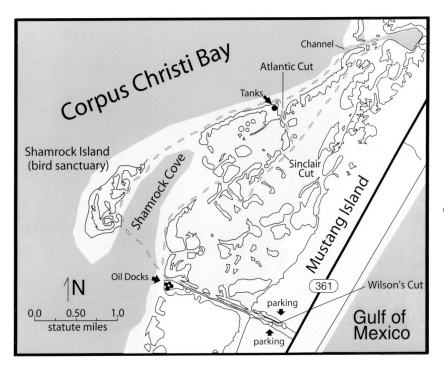

▲ *Wilson's Cut and Shamrock Island. Arrows designate potential routes.*

▶ *Mustang Island State Park, Fish Pass, and Wilson's Cut. Arrows mark the route from Fish Pass to Wilson's Cut.*

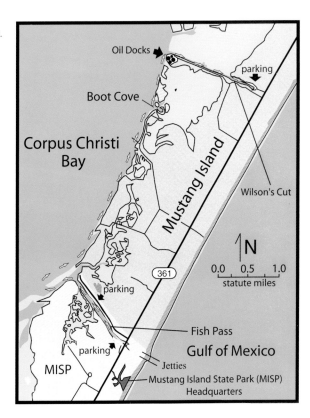

on the west side of the causeway where many birds nest in the spring. If you decide to visit the island, try not to disturb any nesting birds. It is approximately 2 miles from the launch to the *Lexington* and less than 1.5 miles to get to Surfside Park, which is a great place to picnic. Surfside Park is convenient because it has restrooms, tables, and grills. If you decide to paddle in the evening or at night, there is a small crescent beach behind the *Lexington* where you can land and eat outdoors at Pier 99 and listen to live music.

Wilson's Cut and Shamrock Island

BEGINNING TO INTERMEDIATE
9–12 miles

There are two nice loops to paddle on this route: one just under 12 miles and the shorter loop slightly greater than 9 miles. Paddle west-northwest along Wilson's Cut about 1.5 miles (see launch directions for Mustang Island State Park). The marsh along the old pass is good for birdwatching. You will see oil docks and storage tanks on the left at the end of the pass. From here there is an open water crossing of about 1 mile to get to Shamrock Island. Remember, the Nature Conservancy owns this island and landing is not permitted. However, paddling along the island's shoreline offers excellent birdwatching for much of the year. Both resident and migratory species can be observed here. After paddling about 0.75 mile along Shamrock Island, continue with an open water crossing northeast about 0.75 mile and continue along the sandy shoreline of Corpus Christi Bay. These small sandy beaches are an excellent place to picnic, and many people camp here. They also provide a good view of the marshes behind the bay. Continue about 1 mile until you see a small inlet with oil storage tanks. This is Atlantic Cut. For the longer loop continue along the bay another 1.5 miles to the next large inlet. Follow the channel east and turn around behind the bayside island and paddle southwest to reach Sinclair Cut after another 1.5 miles. You can use the tanks at Atlantic Cut as a landmark. Follow Sinclair Cut southwest about 1 mile before turning northwest to reach Shamrock Cove. Paddle back to Wilson's Cut and follow the channel back to the parking area where you started. To take the shorter loop, simply turn south from the bay into Atlantic Cut to reach Sinclair Cut directly.

Fish Pass to Wilson's Cut
BEGINNING TO INTERMEDIATE
6.5–7.5 miles

If you launch from the dirt lot on the south side of Fish Pass (see launch directions for Mustang Island State park), this is approximately a 7.5-mile paddle. If you park and launch at the end of the road along the north side of the pass, the paddle is about 1 mile shorter. A large sand bar is forming along Corpus Christi Bay at the mouth of Fish Pass. As it continues to fill in, it may be necessary to portage over this (see map). The road along the north side of the pass is almost impassable if there has been rain—deep ruts from vehicles getting stuck or digging in serve as a warning. In dry weather there is no problem. Paddling along the shoreline is initially not interesting, but before you see the oil tanks and docks that mark Wilson's Cut, the Boot Cove area is worth exploring and is part of the Nature Conservancy's Francine Cohn Preserve. Also, when you do reach Wilson's Cut, you will see Shamrock Island

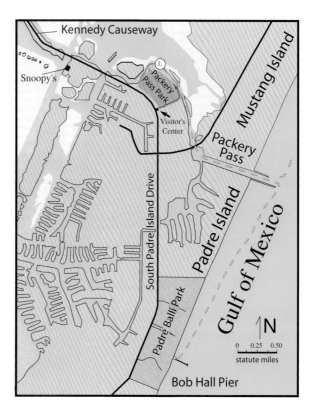

◄ *Padre Balli Park and Packery Pass. L denotes the launch site at Packery Pass Park.*

▼ *Many islands and shell beaches line Corpus Christi Bay and provide quiet places to explore. Photo by Ken Johnson*

◄ *A Caspian tern* (Sterna caspia) *with its prey on Shamrock Island; in the background is a reddish egret* (Egretta rufescens). *Photo by Winifred Shrum*

 Dolphins (Tursiops truncatus) are a common sight while paddling in Corpus Christi Bay. Photo by Ken Johnson

▶ *The beautiful and rare white phase of the reddish egret (Egretta rufescens). The bird has a unique method of "canopy feeding," using its wings to shade the water so as to see the crustaceans and fish on which it feeds. Photo by Winifred Shrum*

less than 1 mile to the northwest, also protected by the Nature Conservancy and a great place to observe birds. However, landing on the island is not permitted.

Packery Channel Park to Padre Balli Park or Mustang Island State Park

INTERMEDIATE TO ADVANCED

9–15 miles

Packery Pass was reopened to the Gulf of Mexico in late 2005. Large jetties now flank the pass in a questionable attempt to keep it open. For paddlers launching from Nueces County's Packery Channel Park, the pass now provides access to the outer coast and developed camping areas north at Mustang Island State Park and south at Nueces County's Padre Balli Park. From the launch paddlers encounter mud flats and sand flats great for birdwatching. Along the waterway are a couple of oak mottes sculptured by the wind. Closer inspection reveals homes built inside. The image gives new meaning to the term *tree house,* but the arrangement moderates the heat in the summer and helps block the wind all year.

Later, take a look at the intertidal zone as you paddle along the jetties. You will see bands of barnacles that correlate with their physiological tolerances. Barnacles are crustaceans that basically glue their heads to the hard substrate and secrete a skeleton made of heavy calcareous plates. Most of their day is

spent opening and closing their plates and kicking their legs from their shell in a mad attempt to filter plankton from the water. Their survival is based on evading predators by living where others cannot live. Their ability to tolerate extremes in temperature and salinity that occur high in the intertidal zone are unsurpassed. Highest on the rocks are *Cthamalus fragilis,* with *Balanus* species below. Toward the ends of the jetties where wave action increases, you may see a cluster or two of the large *Megabalanus,* each specimen about the size of a bowl on the end of a smoker's pipe. You may also observe that the horizontal bands of barnacles expand toward the seaward end of the jetty. A few small mollusks also survive in this zone; the most common have a shield-shaped shell and are called *Siphonaria pectinata.* Although it still has gills, this algae-grazing limpet can use a primitive lung to breath air. It survives desiccation at low tide and evades predators by clamping its shieldlike shell against the rocks. At lower levels are oysters (great to eat) and a variety of intertidal algae. At certain times of the year the

Side Trips
Corpus Christi hosts many interesting area attractions, including the *USS
Lexington* Museum on the bay (800-523-9539,
www.usslexington.com), the Texas State Aquarium (800-477-GULF, www.texasstateaquarium
.org), South Texas Botanical Gardens and
Nature Center (361-852-2100, www.sttxbot.org),
Corpus Christi Museum of Science and History
(361-826-4650, www.ccmuseum.com), and
the Art Museum of South Texas (351-825-3500,
www.artmuseumofsouthtexas.org).

oysters are decimated by stone crabs and other xanthid
crabs. As earlier described, I documented more than five
dozen invertebrate and algae species at Aransas Pass.
The animals and plants provide a huge source of food
for fish. In addition, the passes serve as a bottleneck
where fish must pass to enter and exit the bays. That is
why fishing in the passes is often good all year.

Only more experienced paddlers (or intermediate paddlers accompanied by experienced paddlers)
should venture out into the open Gulf. Depending
on the prevailing winds and currents, taking a trip to
Padre Balli Park to the south or Mustang Island State
Park to the north is fun. The main attraction is surfing
and camping along the beach. If the wind is coming
out of the south or southeast, as it usually does, it is
probably best to go to Padre Balli Park and the Bob
Hall Pier. This is because the most of the work is going
into the wind at the beginning of the trip, followed
by an effortless trip home with the wind. For a day
trip the Bob Hall Pier is a nice destination, as there
is a restaurant (called the Sunset Grill at the time of
writing) at the base of the pier. From Packery Channel
Park paddle about 2 miles to and between the jetties
to reach the Gulf. It is an additional 2.4 miles to get to
Bob Hall Pier at Padre Balli Park for a roundtrip just under 9 miles. Alternatively, it is about 4.5 miles from the
jetties to Mustang Island State Park for a roundtrip of
about 13 miles. The park is just before the Fish Pass jetties. A better approach is to start from Mustang Island

State Park and paddle into the prevailing southeast
winds. Then paddle through Packery Pass 1 mile past
Packery Channel Park under the Kennedy Causeway
to the pier at Snoopy's to eat. The prevailing winds
are usually weaker in the morning and pick up in the
afternoon, so there is less effort going into the wind
in the morning, and you get a big push going home in
the afternoon. The roundtrip distance for this paddle is
approximately 15 miles. ◼

▲▲ *Snoopy's is a tradition
for those paddling along
Packery Pass and Padre
Island National Seashore.
Photo by Ken Johnson*

▲ *The uncommonly
beautiful purple gallinule
(Porphyrula martinica) can
occasionally be seen. Photo
by Carmen Hagopian*

Padre Island National Seashore

This is one of the best paddling destinations in the state of Texas. It offers rough water conditions on the outer coast for experienced paddlers, quiet bayside sand dune communities and salt lagoons to explore and observe wildlife, and access to Mansfield Pass, where dolphins and sea turtles can often be observed. The Padre Island National Seashore occupies the northern half of the island down to Mansfield Pass. Its boundaries also include 11.5 miles of beach south of Mansfield Pass and 18 acres of land donated by the state of Texas along the pass. This barrier island is the longest in the country, stretching 113 miles down the South Texas coast. The western side of the island borders the Upper and Lower Laguna Madre and adjacent Baffin Bay.

Padre Island was originally named Isla Blanca by Alonso Alvarez de Piñeda during his 1519 expedition ordered by Spanish Jamaican Governor Francisco Garay. To this day silver coins are occasionally found at Mansfield Pass, where three out of four Spanish galleons en route from Veracruz to Havana ran aground during a storm. The ships were laden with treasure and a few prominent citizens returning to Spain. Most of the three hundred survivors were killed by Indians or died attempting to return to Mexico. One of the survivors, Francisco Vasquez, returned to the wrecks, where he was rescued three months after the incident by those interested in salvaging the treasure. A large freighter called the *Nicaragua* was wrecked during a storm in 1913 about 10 miles north of Mansfield Pass. The boilers are all that remain and can be seen at extreme low tide. Thanks to legislation introduced by Senator Ralph Yarborough in 1958, the park became officially established in 1962.

Padre Island is named after Padre Nicolas Balli, a Portuguese Catholic priest who obtained a Spanish land grant about 1820 for 50,000 acres on the island, where he and his nephew raised cattle. In the mid to late nineteenth century several ranchers used the island, including John Singer (brother of Isaac Singer of sewing machine fame), Mifflin Kenedy, and Richard King. In 1879 Patrick Dunn began leasing land on the island, and by 1926 the "Duke of Padre" owned almost the entire island. He built line camps up and down the island at 15-mile intervals for rounding up cattle. Despite the harsh conditions, the Novillo Line Camp still exists on the northern side of the island, although it is not accessible to visitors.

Padre Island National Seashore is on the northern part of the island and is accessible by car for only a few miles southeast of Corpus Christi. Vehicle access is $10, and camping is in five designated areas. Bayside access and camping can be found just inside the park at Bird Island Basin or about 20 miles south at Yarborough Pass. There is access all along the Gulf of Mexico side of the island but camping is allowed only at North Beach, Malaquite Beach, and South Beach. South Beach

The national seashore occupies the northern half of the 113-mile-long Padre Island. Some of the dunes are fascinating to explore. Photo by Ken Johnson

provides access to Mansfield Pass, but requires four-wheel-drive beyond the 5-mile marker (South Beach is approximately 60 miles long). For all camping permits and information, stop in at the Malaquite Visitor Center a few miles inside the park.

Recommended Navigational Aids

Padre Island National Seashore, Texas #251, by Trails Illustrated; *Lower Laguna Madre* waterproof map by Hook-N-Line Map Company; aerial maps downloaded from TerraServer (www.terraserver.com), Google Earth (http://earth.google.com), or MapQuest (www.mapquest.com).

Planning Considerations

No landing is permitted on the dredge spoil islands or North or South Bird Island from February 1 to August 31, so that nesting birds are not disturbed. Paddlers launching from Bird Island Basin must pay a user fee at the park entrance or visitor center. If your intended destination is down South Beach or to Mansfield or Yarborough Pass, you need a four-wheel-drive vehicle. South Beach is

Bayside sunset at Padre Island National Seashore.

60 miles long and the park requires four-wheel-drive beyond mile marker 5. Mile markers are at 5-mile intervals to provide a reference for visitors and rangers. It is wise to carry extra fuel. Also, check your tide tables. It is faster and easier to drive down the beach at low tide. During very high tides, motorists may become temporarily stranded or be forced to drive high on the beach where the sand is soft and even a four-wheel-drive vehicle may become stranded. A shovel and a board or two are useful when driving in these areas in case you become stranded, as help may not be readily available. Just before the 15-mile marker down South Beach is the turn-off for Yarborough Pass, where there is a bayside campground. Sand accumulates at the entrance to the bayside road, and even a four-wheel-drive without significant clearance may have trouble getting through this soft sand. The road is often closed because of flooding or oil company activities, so call the park to get an update before embarking on a trip. For emergencies call park headquarters during normal operating hours at 361-949-8173 extension 0. Otherwise call 911. For local outfitting or to be dropped off or picked up, call Ken Johnson in Corpus Christi at 361-855-3926 or contact him by e-mail at johnsonkw@earthlink.net.

Accommodations

Only primitive camping is allowed in the park. There are numerous accommodations outside the park at Corpus Christi (Corpus Christi Convention and Visitor's Bureau, 800-678-OCEAN, http://corpuschristicvb.com). One of my favorites because of proximity to the park is the Best Western On The Island (14050 S. Padre Island Drive, Corpus Christi, TX 78418–6026, 361-949-2300). If camping in the park, obtain a permit from the park entrance or Malaquite visitor center. If doing day trips, it is usually best to camp on the outer coast, where onshore breezes keep you cool and there are fewer mosquitoes. Malaquite Beach has designated sites with picnic tables, a rinse shower, and toilet facilities. North Beach, South Beach, and Yarborough Pass offer primitive camping with no facilities. The Bird Island Basin camping area has chemical toilets and some picnic tables but is otherwise undeveloped. For more details, see the official website for the park (http://www.nps.gov/pais/index.htm).

Directions to Launch Sites

Padre Island National Seashore: To access Bird Island Basin drive south into Padre Island National Seashore and turn right at the sign off Park Road 22 approximately 2–3 miles past the park entrance. Follow the road to the bayshore. If you are paddling north, turn right at the sign for the public boat ramp. If you are heading south to the Green Hill dune field, Yarborough Pass, or Baffin Bay, then continue to the camping or windsurfing area directly ahead and launch from the beach.

If you are interested in surfing on the outer coast, you can drive down the beach, find a secluded place, and launch anywhere. The access road to North Beach is just inside the park. Malaquite Beach and visitor center are between North and South beaches. To get to South Beach, you follow Park Road 22 to its terminus on the beach. South Beach extends 60 miles from the end of the road. As you drive south there are mile markers posted at 5-mile intervals. Four-wheel-drive vehicles are required beyond the 5-mile marker (see Planning Considerations). To get to Yarborough Pass, drive down South Beach and turn right just before the 15-mile marker. This road is often blocked by soft sand, so check with park staff beforehand to ensure the road is open. Drive across the island past some oil or gas wells to reach a small parking lot and boat launching area along the north side of the pass, or continue to the end of the road to camp and launch off the beach (see map, p. 114). To get to Mansfield Pass, drive 60 miles down South Beach to the jetty. Either paddle through the surf and out around the jetty into the pass, or carry boats to the inside beach along the north side of the pass. The easiest way to get boats to the inside beach is to carry them up along the jetty adjacent to the beach, then follow the road along the channel approximately 100 yards to a small protected beach.

The Outer Coast

ADVANCED PADDLERS, SURFING ONLY

Since most of the outer coast is accessible by four-wheel-drive along the national seashore, you can drive to your camping destination and surf or paddle along the shore wherever you wish. However, realize

The sands of Padre with the common sand dollar (Mellita quinquiesperforata). *Sand dollar beds form extensive nearshore communities all along the Texas coast.*

that help is not readily available, and surf conditions along the coast can be deceiving. As discussed in the introduction, when the surf is up, the surf zone can extend far offshore. From the beach it may look like a 3- foot break, but farther out it really could be 4 to 7 feet. This can happen because wave troughs farther from shore may not be visible, and more distant waves look smaller. Careful observation of wave sets is imperative. Watch for rips for entry and take some time to observe wave trains for larger and more dangerous wave sets.

Since prevailing winds and waves are typically out of the southeast, the Mansfield Pass jetties often form a sheltered area in the waters just north of the jetties that can be used to access the pass or paddle out to surf farther up the beach. However, beware of wave refraction off the jetties, which can cause confused seas and difficult paddling conditions.

▲ Clumps of vegetation trap sand to develop coppice dunes along the back island sand flat.

▶ The keeled earless lizard (Holbrookia propinqua) is a common resident of the Padre Island dunes.

▲ Bird Island Basin. Arrows signify potential routes around North and South Bird Islands.

 ### Bird Island Basin Shoreline

BEGINNING

1–3 miles

To paddle south along the shore, launch from the windsurfing area. To paddle north, launch from the boat ramp area (see Directions to Launch Sites). There are sandy beaches here and the water is usually clear. Birdwatching is often good along the shore and there are several dune fields along the shoreline that can be explored. The most interesting dune field is approximately 1–1.5 miles north of the boat ramp.

South Bird Island Loop

INTERMEDIATE

4 miles

With good birdwatching and interesting sand dune formations, this short loop is one of my favorite trips along the coast. Looking from the Bird Island Basin boat ramp, a line of islands is visible to the northwest. Most of them line the eastern side of the intracoastal waterway. The waterway's large pilings and barge traffic make a good point of reference. Paddle north-northwest to the first island, but avoid the sand bar that extends southeast from the first island. In general this short chain of islands extends northeast. Follow the eastern shorelines to see birds. You can paddle into some of the small coves and inlets (see map) to get a closer look, but do not disturb the birds, and obey the signs that prohibit landing on the islands from February 1 to August 31. A good pair of binoculars or spotting scope is useful for birdwatching. The chain of islands is approximately 1.5 miles long. At the end of the chain is South Bird Island. At the north end of this island turn and paddle southeast back to the Padre Island shoreline. Here there is a large sand dune complex with seasonal freshwater ponds. This is an interesting place to observe sand dune formations and wildlife, but be careful not to trample the plants or dunes. Continue southwest along the shoreline to complete the loop and return to the boat ramp.

North Bird Island Loop

INTERMEDIATE

9 miles

This is an extension of the South Bird Island Loop. Follow the route above to reach South Bird Island. From South Bird Island there is an open water crossing less than a mile north-northeast to reach a second small chain of islands along the intracoastal waterway. Paddle northeast along the islands' eastern shorelines. Again this is a great place to birdwatch. About a mile up the eastern shoreline of the island chain (on your left), you will see North Bird Island on your right. Remember, landing on any of the small islands is prohibited from February 1 to August 31. Paddle between the islands and around North Bird Island before heading south back to the sandy shoreline of Padre Island. Behind the sandy shoreline is a series of large brackish ponds where flocks of ducks and other birds can be observed during the winter. Continue past the shoreline sand dune complex noted in the preceding route description to return to the Bird Island Basin boat ramp.

Green Hill Dune Field

BEGINNING TO INTERMEDIATE

10 miles

This is one of the best examples of a back island sand dune field on the Texas coast. Launch from the beach

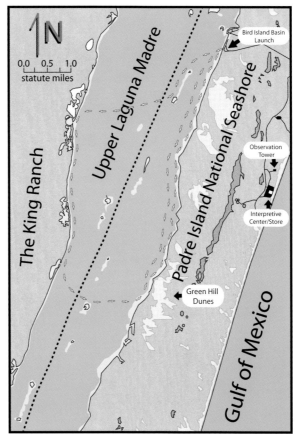

▲ Many seasonally flooded freshwater pools provide a water supply for wildlife living on the island.

◀ Padre Island National Seashore from Bird Basin to the Green Hill dunes. Arrows mark potential routes to the Green Hill dunes from the King Ranch shoreline.

▲ A wind-proof tent, a solid rain fly, and a set of long, angled sand stakes are useful when camping in the dunes, where high winds and scattered thunderstorms are common.

▲ Sand can accumulate to form large bayside dunes. The Green Hill dune formation a few miles south of the Bird Island Basin is a good example. Photo by Ken Johnson

▶ When lightning strikes a sand dune it melts the sand together in interesting patterns called fulgurites. This was found at the top of a large dune on the bay side of the island. Photo by Ken Johnson

at the Bird Island Basin windsurfing and camping area and follow the shoreline south. You will notice that the water is clear and shallow over sand close to shore. The bottom slopes to 2 or 3 feet deep at the edge of the sea grass meadows approximately 50 to 100 yards from shore. You can tell where the sand ends and the sea grass begins as the water turns a dark color. For ease of paddling, you need to be at least this far from shore. On clear water days, snorkeling along the edge of the sea grass meadows can be interesting. There are some small dune fields with a few scattered, marshy ponds where birds and other wildlife may be seen.

Approximately 5 miles down the shore is the large Green Hill dune complex, which extends for more than a mile. One of the dunes reaches to the water's edge. This is your destination. From here you can hike to explore the dune field. Be careful not to trample plants or dunes. There is a freshwater spring in the vicinity and several freshwater ponds and marshes support a variety of wildlife, including birds, deer, and coyotes. The dune formations are incredible! Paddle north-northeast back along the shoreline to return to the Bird Island Basin.

The King Ranch/Green Hill Dune Field Loop

INTERMEDIATE TO ADVANCED

15.5 miles

For the more adventurous and fit, this route is an excellent loop around the bay. Launch from the beach at the Bird Island Basin windsurfing and camping area. Paddle southwest and then south-southwest parallel to the intracoastal waterway, but stay approximately 0.25 mile east of the waterway. Approximately 1.5 to 1.75 miles out you will come across a small island. There may be many birds on the island, and remember, you cannot land there from February 1 to August 31. From the island, paddle open water approximately 2 miles west-southwest to the King Ranch shoreline. Congratulations, you have crossed the Upper Laguna Madre! A couple of shallow salt lagoons that open into the bay at high tides offer good birdwatching and occasionally good fishing. Follow the shoreline approximately 4 miles south to the opening of another salt lagoon. From here on clear days you may be able to see rising above the horizon the Green Hill dunes and a small island between you and the opposite shoreline. Paddle southeast approximately 1 mile to the small island and then another 1.25–1.5 miles due east to reach the Green Hill dune complex on Padre Island National Seashore. Land where part of the dune field forms a beach (see preceding route for a description of the dune field). Paddle north-northeast back along the shoreline 5 miles to reach the Bird Island Basin to finish the loop.

Yarborough Pass

INTERMEDIATE TO ADVANCED

variable mileages

From 1941 to 1944 four attempts were made to create a pass through Padre Island to the Upper Laguna Madre. Each time the pass quickly filled in with sand. The last effort to open Yarborough Pass was in 1952. Within three weeks the pass some 60 feet wide had shrunk to only 6 feet across, and within three months it was closed again. A small portion of the pass is navigable and a boat ramp and campground are located on the bay side of the island. Drive down South Beach to the 15-mile marker. Just before the 15-mile marker is the road across the foredunes to Yarborough Pass. The sand here can be treacherous, even for four-wheel-drive vehicles. Once you cross the soft sand of the foredunes, the road is usually good. Call ahead before planning to use this road, as it is occasionally closed due to flooding. Drive along the road past some gas wells, then along the old pass to a small boat launch where there is a parking area. If you are camping, continue to the end of the road, where a concrete picnic table signals the designated primitive camping area. You can also launch from the beach here.

When the water or tide is high, there are some interesting dune fields accessible south of the pass. You can access the mouth of Baffin Bay from here, but finding your way back may be difficult because of the lack of landmarks. Good compass skills and a GPS are useful here for navigation. The area is not especially engaging in itself, but I have used this camping area on a two-day 44-mile trip from Riviera Beach in Baffin Bay to the Bird Island Basin. On my first attempt I was unable to find the Yarborough Pass camping area and was forced to camp on a spoil island after the sun went down. It is safest to use the intracoastal waterway to avoid getting stuck on shallow bars in this area. The distance to the Bird Island Basin is approximately 20.5 miles. For an experienced kayaker, it is good to do a trip from here to the Bird Island Basin to become familiar with the area before attempting the longer Baffin Bay to Bird Island Basin trip. Another approach would be to paddle to Baffin Bay's Riviera Beach (approximately 23.5 miles) and back, staying overnight in one of the lodges (see Baffin Bay accommodations). Obviously, at 47 miles, this is quite an undertaking and should be attempted only by experienced and fit paddlers already familiar with the area and its landmarks and navigation (see map, p. 114).

Mansfield Pass

INTERMEDIATE TO ADVANCED

1–6 miles

This area offers great fishing, good chances for observing sea turtles and dolphins, and interesting dune

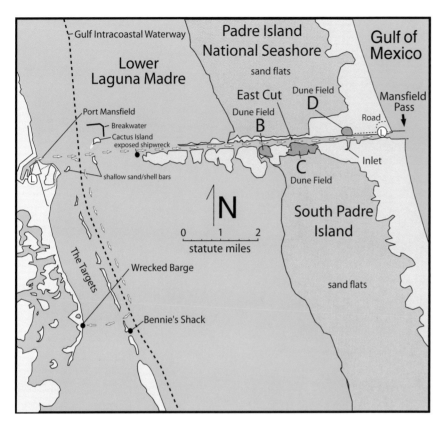

Map labels:
Gulf Intracoastal Waterway
Padre Island National Seashore
Gulf of Mexico
Lower Laguna Madre
sand flats
East Cut
Dune Field
Mansfield Pass
Port Mansfield
Dune Field
Breakwater
Road
Cactus Island
exposed shipwreck
Inlet
shallow sand/shell bars
Dune Field
N
0   1   2
statute miles
South Padre Island
The Targets
Wrecked Barge
sand flats
Bennie's Shack

fields and flats with abundant wildlife. Drive 60 miles down South Beach. Remember that four-wheel-drive is mandatory and it is best to drive at low tides. Drive to the jetty that flanks the north side of Mansfield Pass. If the weather is calm, or you are experienced with surf and nearshore currents, you can launch from the beach and paddle out and around the north jetty into Mansfield Pass. The safer way is to portage kayaks to a small beach behind the jetty along the channel. There is a concrete picnic table at the base of the jetty adjacent to the beach. Behind the jetty along the channel that forms Mansfield Pass is a dirt road that extends 0.75 mile west to a dune field along the channel. The road that follows the channel can sometimes be accessed by driving up next to the jetty or via another access road starting about 0.3 mile north up the Gulf beach and circling around to intersect the channel road. However, soft sand can strand even the best

four-wheel-drive vehicle, and unless the channel has recently been dredged, the access adjacent to the jetty is too steep and rocky to pass. You can make a short portage by walking up on the jetty and west along the road, where you can launch from a sandy beach along the channel.

Once in the channel, watch for turtle heads popping up. Sea turtles are common here. Most are green sea turtles, but other species have been sighted. If paddling around the end of the jetties you may also see tarpon. Look for their large silvery-scaled backs exposed in the troughs of large waves near the end of the jetties. Occasionally the water may be clear enough inside the pass adjacent to the jetties to invite snorkeling. Less than 1 mile west along the pass is a small dune field on the north side of the channel (see *D* on map). Since it is part of the national seashore, no camping is allowed here, but it is a rewarding place to hike. Avoid trampling the vegetation and dunes. Across the channel from this field are two interesting inlets to explore or fish at high tide. The birdwatching is often excellent here.

There are two more dune fields on the south side of the channel approximately 2 and 3 miles respectively from the jetties. The first is one of the largest fields accessible on the Texas coast and well worth a visit, while the second has some interesting vegetation (see *B* and *C* on map). If you hike south through these fields, you will come out on the sand flats that line the back part of Padre Island. Large transverse dunes give way to smaller barchan dunes and then sand flats as far as the eye can see. It can be hard to tell where the extensive sand flats behind Padre Island end and where the water begins. Distances are deceiving and the views are surreal. In the channel between these two large dune fields, dolphins can almost always be observed. Unlike elsewhere on the coast, here these animals often approach kayakers. I have seen them perform incredible acrobatics after a cold front or thunderstorm has passed through. The best places to camp are on the outer coast adjacent to the jetties. For maps and additional information on Mansfield Pass or Port Mansfield, see the section entitled Port Mansfield.

■

Surfing the outer coast is fun and never crowded along South Beach, a 60-mile beach that extends south to Mansfield Pass. Most of the beach is accessible only with four-wheel-drive vehicles.

Baffin Bay

THE Baffin Bay area provides sea kayakers with challenging conditions along undeveloped shorelines abundant with wildlife. Baffin Bay extends west from the Upper Laguna Madre to connect with several tertiary embayments, including Alazan Bay, Laguna Salada, and Cayo del Grullo. Although Santa Gertrudis, Olmos, and San Fernando creeks provide some freshwater inflow during periods of rainfall, there is no substantial river flowing into any of these bays. Surprisingly, Baffin Bay is a relatively deep bay for Texas. Although it is a secondary bay, its average depth exceeds that of the adjacent primary bay, Upper Laguna Madre.

The only significant hard substrate on the Texas coast is produced by oyster reefs except in this bay and part of Upper Laguna Madre. Here, when your boat scrapes the

The shoreline in Baffin Bay is a combination of grassland and cactus with few trees.

bottom, it will often be on serpulid reefs. These poly-chaete worms live in calcareous tubes and form large colonies. Their tentacles can extend from the opening of each tube to serve as gills and to collect food suspended in the water column. They are hardy little animals that can survive huge fluctuations in salinity occurring because of evaporation and the lack of freshwater inflow. The salinity in Baffin Bay can exceed 50–60 parts per thousand (open ocean averages approximately 35 ppt). This fact alone may limit the number and diversity of predators that can feed on these worms.

Salinity may also be the reason why Baffin Bay may be the origin for brown tides created by the small algae *Aureoumbra lagunensis.* According to the Texas Parks and Wildlife Department, 200 of the single-celled algae could fit side by side on the head of a pin and there can be 1–2 million cells in a single milliliter of water during a bloom. Unlike red tides produced by dinoflagellates, these algae are harmless to people, and blooms may be part of a natural cycle. However, blooms can devastate sea grass meadows by blocking out light, and they also diminish zooplankton important to the fish and invertebrates that feed on them.

Most of the Baffin Bay shoreline is lined with sandy or shell beaches with small inlets into small salt lagoons that are excellent for birdwatching. A few are very good for fishing as well. The tertiary bays Cayo del Grullo, Laguna Salada, and Alazan Bay are muddy, but some of the erosion patterns on the mudstone bluffs with overhanging cactus are beautiful. Nilgai antelope, deer, javelinas, and feral pigs are often spotted from the shoreline. At times the fishing for redfish and sea trout is unbelievable. Riviera Beach and Loyola Beach provide the only public access to this interesting area. These two small retirement communities are situated on a peninsula that separates Cayo del Grullo from Laguna Salada on the west end of Baffin Bay.

The King Ranch borders the northern shoreline of the bay complex, while the Kenedy Ranch borders the south. Richard King and lifelong friend and business mentor Mifflin Kenedy met during the Seminole War in Florida, working on steamboats. They transferred their service to the Rio Grande during the Mexican-American War, and the steamboat company they founded after the war dominated Rio Grande trade for more than two decades. As their profits grew, King and Kenedy began buying up land in the 1850s and formed their ranching partnership in 1860. In 1868 they dissolved this partnership to separate their ranches. The two men ultimately acquired millions of acres of what was known as the Wild Horse Desert. La Parra Ranch, including the old family home and former center of operations for the Kenedy family, is 6 miles east of the small town of Sarita on Highway 77. After Sarita Kenedy East died, La Parra Ranch was donated to the Mission Oblates of Mary Immaculate, a French Catholic organization that had visited and served the ranch since the late 1800s. Still run by the Oblates, it is now called Lebh Shomea House of Prayer, serves as a religious retreat, and has nature trails on 1,000 acres, including 10 acres along Baffin Bay's southern shore. The King family home and ranch headquarters are near Kingsville. Both families have historical museums, and the King Ranch gives tours and allows hunting on its property (see Side Trips).

In 1907 Theodore Koch bought a strip of land from the King Ranch and founded the towns of Riviera and Riviera Beach on Baffin Bay. He attempted to establish a resort at Riviera Beach, but his attempts were thwarted by a seven-year drought and a severe hurricane. The boat ramp between the Baffin Bay Café and Kratz Bait Camp store in Riviera Beach provides paddlers with the best access to Baffin Bay and the Laguna Salada (see Directions to Launch Sites). The Kratz Bait Camp store has been a fixture in Riviera Beach for more than fifty years. The owner's son is a fantastic chef who operates the adjacent Baffin Bay Café. Just to the north, local farmer Orlando Underbrink bought waterfront property in 1935, where he built a small resort with café, grocery store, and fishing pier. This eventually became the town of Loyola Beach, named after his father Ignatius Loyola Underbrink. Orlando's café is now known as King's Inn, a popular seafood restaurant made famous by patrons such as baseball great Nolan Ryan, politician George W. Bush, and country western singer George Strait. Kleberg County built Kaufer-Hubert Memorial Park south of Loyola Beach in 1955. The small park has an observation tower, a playground, picnic facilities under large shady mesquite trees, a sandy beach, public boat ramp, and fishing pier. The adjacent Seawind RV Park is the best tent camping and RV facility in the area. The Loyola Beach area provides sea kayakers with excellent access to the Cayo del Grullo and Baffin Bay.

Recommended Navigational Aids

Padre Island National Seashore, Texas #251, by Trails Illustrated; *Lower Laguna Madre* and *Upper Laguna Madre* waterproof maps by Shoreline Publishing; aerial maps downloaded from TerraServer (www.terraserver.com), Google Earth (http://earth.google.com), or MapQuest (www.mapquest.com).

Planning Considerations

Avoid paddling the upper reaches of the Laguna Salada, Cayo del Grullo, and Alazan Bay during very low tides. When there are moderate to strong winds out of the southeast, avoid paddling from Kleberg Point across the mouth of Alazan Bay. There is a significant fetch from the southeast bend of Baffin Bay to Kleberg Point across relatively deep water. These wind-generated waves can become very large and refract off the low mudstone bluff along the southeast shore of Kleberg Point, creating confused seas and often a standing wave pattern called clapotis, which can be dangerous. However, for strong and experienced paddlers, this area can be challenging and fun. If paddling through Baffin Bay to the upper Laguna Madre, it is best to follow the southern shoreline of Baffin Bay. Carry a cell phone and be prepared to contact one of the local guides to transport you back to Riviera or Loyola Beach if there are thunderstorms or sudden changes in conditions. In case of emergency, they also may be the closest and best option for assistance, or help may be obtained from the Kenedy County sheriff in Sarita at 512-294-5205. A listing of most fishing guides is available online (www.baffinbaytx.com/fishingguides.htm).

Accommodations

In Riviera Beach the Baffin Bay Lodge (361–297–5555, www.baffinbaylodge.com) and Baffin on the Rocks (361-592-3474, www.baffinontherocks.com) are the best places to stay. For information on food, lodging, and guide services, see the website www.baffinbaytx

.com. South of Loyola Beach, the Sea Wind RV Resort is the best place for tent camping and RVs, but phone reservations are not accepted (361-297-5738). The facility is adjacent to Kaufer-Hubert Memorial Park, which is the nicest place to launch and land on the peninsula. Showers and a laundromat are available and pets are allowed. For those willing to spend a little more money, the Baffin Bay Inn near Loyola Beach is a nice place with kitchenettes, providing kayakers with a place to launch and land and with fresh water to clean gear (361-297-5158). As earlier noted, two excellent restaurants on the peninsula are the Baffin Bay Café and King's Inn.

Directions to Launch Sites

Riviera Beach: Find the boat ramp at Kratz Bait Camp in Riviera Beach for the most direct access to Baffin Bay and for those interested in crossing the bay to reach the Upper Laguna Madre. Travel from the north or south on Highway 77 to the town of Riviera. Turn east on FM 771 and travel about 8–9 miles to reach Riviera Beach. Toward the end of the road, stay right until you see the Baffin Bay Café. The Kratz Bait Camp store and the boat ramp are next to it. The café has a nice wooden patio and dock facility where paddlers and other boaters are welcome to come and eat. To access the upper Laguna Salada, which is extremely shallow, you can turn south off FM 771 onto FM 2510 south. When FM 2510 takes a 90-degree left turn to the east, continue south or straight ahead on a small road that takes you to a sandy and muddy trail along the shoreline. Follow the road east along the shore to get to the best spot to launch. I have seen the locals cross the Laguna Salada with high clearance four-wheel-drive vehicles occasionally at very low tides, using the path of the telephone poles that cross this small bay. I do not recommend trying this!

Kaufer-Hubert Memorial Park: To access Baffin Bay and the Cayo del Grullo, just south of Loyola Beach is Kleberg County's Kaufer-Hubert Memorial Park, the nicest place to launch on the peninsula. The park has a small birding trail and bird observation tower, a small sandy beach with freshwater shower, and parking area with a public boat ramp. Picnic and playground facilities are under large mesquite trees that provide ample shade. Travel north from Brownsville or south from

Side Trips
The Kenedy Ranch Museum is located in the town of Sarita, slightly more than 20 miles south of Kingsville and just off U.S. Highway 77 (361-294-5751, www.kenedyranch museum.org). The King Ranch Museum is located at 405 North 6th Street in Kingsville, and the King Ranch Visitor Center is west of Kingsville on Highway 141 (361-592-8055, www.king-ranch.com). Lebh Shomea House of Prayer is on the old Kenedy estate or La Parra Ranch (361-294-5369, www.lebhshomea.org).

Kingsville on Highway 77 to get to FM 628 a few miles north of the town of Riviera. Turn east on FM 628 approximately 8 miles past the old community of Vattmannville to Loyola Beach. Follow the road south along the shore past the small bridge that crosses Vattmann Creek. Kaufer-Hubert Memorial Park can be seen to the left as you cross the bridge, and the entrance to this and the Seawind RV Park is just south of the bridge.

Cayo del Grullo
INTERMEDIATE
5.5–9.5 miles

If you have little time or are not in great shape, this trip offers a fair overview of Baffin Bay. Launch from Kaufer-Hubert Memorial Park and make an open water crossing east-northeast approximately 1.75 miles across the Cayo del Grullo to the King Ranch shoreline. As you approach the shore, you will see a sandy spit adjacent to a salt lagoon (see map). On higher tides it is possible to paddle into the lagoon behind the spit. Paddle north-northwest along the spit across the lagoon. As you approach the north end of the lagoon, look for the deeper channel adjacent to the shoreline opposite the spit to get back into the bay. The lagoon is a great place to watch birds. Paddle past another lagoon too shallow to navigate and you will see another sand/shell spit that extends northwest from the shore-

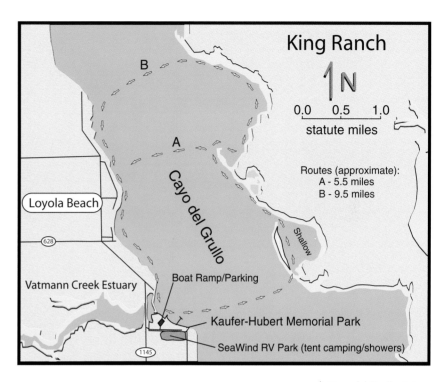

▲ Cayo del Grullo. Letters and arrows mark potential routes. With camping nearby, Kaufer-Hubert Memorial Park provides good access to the bay and a shady park for a picnic.

◄ The eroded mudstone bluffs of the Cayo del Grullo and parts of the Baffin Bay shoreline are different than anywhere else on the coast.

▶ *Baffin Bay to the Upper Laguna Madre. Launch sites at Loyola and Riviera Beach are numbered. Padre Island National Seashore is also shown, with Yarborough Pass and the Green Hill dunes.*

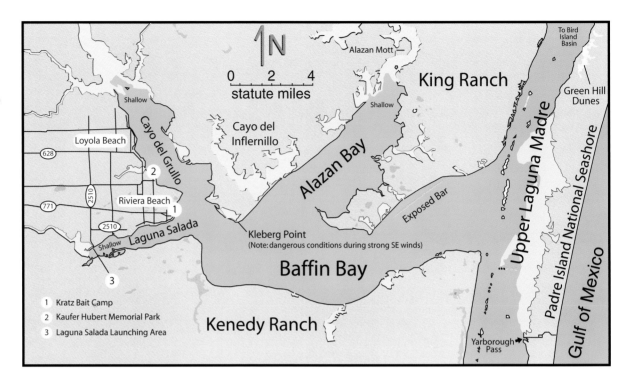

▼ *Kleberg Point is accessible from the boat ramp located next to Kratz Bait Camp. The water east of Kleberg Point can be very rough when prevailing winds are strongly out of the southeast. This is made more complicated by wave refraction off the mudstone bluffs on the east side of the point.*

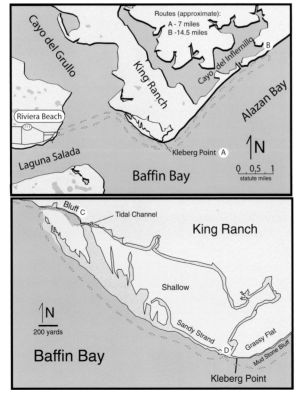

line. Pelicans and shorebirds usually congregate along and at the end of this spit. As you approach the end of the spit you can either paddle back across the bay due west or paddle east around the end of the spit and back to the King Ranch shoreline. If you paddle back across the bay, you can follow the opposite shoreline southeast back past Loyola Beach to the park where you began your 5.5-mile journey. If you have a few minutes and the tide is not too low, it is fun to paddle around the mouth of the Vattmann Creek estuary adjacent to the park to do some birdwatching.

If you opt for the longer 9.5-mile route, travel north along the King Ranch shoreline after paddling east around the spit. Colorful mudstone or clay bluffs have eroded into interesting formations with large stands of prickly pear cactus. Follow the shoreline until it begins heading west-northwest before paddling back across the bay to the southwest to reach the opposite shore. Paddle south past Loyola Beach back to Kaufer-Hubert Memorial Park where you began.

Kleberg Point Route

INTERMEDIATE TO ADVANCED

7, 14.5, and 23 miles

This can be one of the most dangerous and difficult trips along the coast or it can be one of the easiest, depending on the weather. If prevailing winds are out of the east or southeast, a significant fetch exists over a relatively deep bay. This can result in choppy conditions on the initial open water crossing and occasionally large breaking waves past Kleberg Point. Wave refraction against the low mudstone bluff along the eastern side of Kleberg Point can result in confused seas and even clapotis at the mouth of Alazan Bay. I have been out when the waves and wind coming out of the southeast were so strong that after an hour of paddling from Kleberg Point, I was unable to cross the mouth of Alazan Bay. I began to feel seasick and lose my balance and strength after swallowing a good deal of seawater while crashing into the oncoming waves in high winds. Realizing that I was making little headway against the wind and waves, I turned around and surfed back to Riviera Beach in less than thirty-five minutes.

Launch from the boat ramp adjacent to the Kratz Bait Camp store and paddle 1.75–2 miles east-northeast to the King Ranch shoreline. Follow the shoreline southeast toward Kleberg Point. There is a small salt lagoon enclosed by a sand spit. You can follow close to the shoreline inside the sand spit to find a channel that goes into the lagoon. Use your paddle tips to feel the bottom and find the channel. At higher tides you can paddle along the shore at the back of the lagoon to find a salt creek where there is often good fishing. At very high tides you can paddle up the creek into an even bigger lagoon where there is an exit near Kleberg Point. However, this is risky at best, so I would not recommend it. Paddling back out of the creek into the smaller lagoon and around the spit is the best way to go.

Continue paddling southeast toward Kleberg Point, where you can rest on an intertidal spit of coarse sand and shell. From here you can see the larger salt lagoon already described. On Kleberg Point in the intertidal zone are often large numbers of hermit crabs occupy-

ing large moon snail and lightning whelk shells. Other large debris present is a clue that this point receives significant wave exposure and is at the end of a long fetch extending to the southeast. To limit the trip to 7 miles, return from Kleberg Point to Riviera Beach.

If the conditions are calm or you are skilled, paddle around Kleberg Point and along the mudstone bluff about 1 mile into the mouth of Alazan Bay for a longer route (14 miles). As you paddle northeast along the shoreline, you will begin to see one of the largest salt lagoons along the Texas coast, the Cayo del Infiernillo. Large flocks of birds congregate seasonally inside this lagoon, and there is usually a gathering of seabirds along a sandy inlet that opens into the middle of the lagoon. All fish that move into or out of this lagoon must pass through this small inlet, making it a popular area for birds such as pelicans to congregate. During high tides you can paddle into the shallow lagoon, where flocks of birds feed on invertebrates. If you can get permission from the King Ranch, there is a grassy bluff above a shell beach suitable for landing on the east side of the lagoon. Notice how small and fine the shells are on this beach in comparison with those at Kleberg Point. These small clams deposited in the intertidal zone are from Alazan Bay, where conditions are calmer, sediments are finer, and the assemblage of clams and other invertebrates is significantly different. Paddle back to Kleberg Point. Less experienced paddlers can follow the shoreline northwest before making the open water crossing to Riviera Beach. More experienced paddlers can paddle directly from Kleberg Point to Riviera Beach. If the wind and waves are coming out of the southeast, it can be quite a ride!

A variation for very fit and experienced paddlers is to set a heading from Riviera directly to Kleberg Point and then to East Kleberg Point across the mouth of Alazan Bay. As you are crossing Alazan Bay you will see remnants of a long pier extending from the opposite shoreline. Beyond East Kleberg Point are some nice sandy beaches toward the mouth of Baffin Bay. Birdwatching can be great in several salt lagoons behind these beaches. A long sand bar called Tide Gauge Bar parallels this shoreline for several miles. The water in this area is often clear, and the flat between the bar and the shoreline is a great place to fish for sea trout and redfish. Paddle back southwest to East Kleberg Point and then west past Kleberg Point to Riviera Beach.

Laguna Salada to Kratz Bait Camp or Kaufer-Hubert Memorial Park

BEGINNING TO INTERMEDIATE

4–8 miles

Launch at the Laguna Salada shoreline off FM 2510 (see Directions to Launch Sites) on the south side of the peninsula. Remember when you reach the shoreline you can drive east along the shore on an unpaved road to reach the best place to launch. This road may not be passable if conditions are wet or the tide is high.

If there is any question, scout the road first. Paddle east along the shoreline past the county fishing pier to the boat ramp between Kratz Bait Camp store and the Baffin Bay Café to land. If taking the longer route, continue paddling past Riviera Beach north and west around the peninsula until you reach Kaufer-Hubert Memorial Park, where you can land either on the beach or at the public boat ramp. If taking the longer route, the Baffin Bay Café makes a nice lunch stop. Remember that these areas are shallow and may not be passable at very low tides.

There are some long day trips and multiday trips from Padre Island National Seashore into Baffin Bay. See the section on Padre Island National Seashore for additional information. ▮

Port Mansfield

PORT Mansfield provides sea kayakers with access to the most interesting parts of the Lower Laguna Madre, including the bay side of central and southern Padre Island and Mansfield Pass. Originally part of the San Juan Carracitos land grant, Port Mansfield was acquired by Captain Richard King in 1880. For more than fifty years, it was merely a fishing beach along the bay side of the Lower Laguna Madre and was called Redfish Landing. In 1933 the land was leased to the local American Legion Post for recreational purposes by the executors of Mrs. King's estate. At that time a road was built and the land comprising Redfish Landing was subdivided for development. In 1948 the Willacy County Navigation District (WCND) was formed to exploit the county's access to the Lower Laguna Madre and the Gulf of Mexico. The WCND acquired 1,760 acres around Redfish Landing in 1950 and renamed the area Port Mansfield after the Texas legislator responsible for

Several large sand dune fields line Mansfield Pass.

▲ *Looking down across Mansfield Pass from one of the larger dunes.*

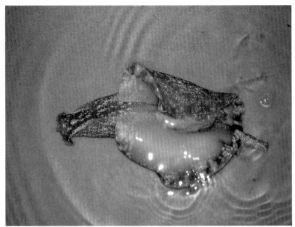

▲ *The sea hare* (Aplysia brasiliana) *is an important herbivore that feeds primarily on sea grass.*

▲ *Great care must be taken when paddling in the open Gulf of Mexico, especially in isolated areas like Mansfield Pass*

extending the Gulf Intracoastal Waterway from Corpus Christi to Brownsville. In 1954 work began to dredge a channel from Port Mansfield to the Gulf of Mexico through Padre Island. Granite jetties flanking the channel into the Gulf were constructed by the U.S. Army Corps of Engineers in 1962. When the channel was being dredged, gold and silver Spanish doubloons were discovered. It is thought the treasure may have originated from the Spanish ships *Espíritu Santo, San Esteban* and *Santa María de Yciar,* which were part of a twenty-ship fleet that departed Vera Cruz for Spain in 1553. Of their more than three hundred passengers and crews, only two people survived the storm and shipwreck to tell their story.

Fortunately, the King Ranch and other private landholders have largely prevented industrial development in the area around Port Mansfield, which means this part of the coast is comparatively pristine. Commercial oil and fishing industries no longer make much use of the port as they did in the 1970s and 1980s. The town is primarily known for recreational fishing and hunting and has fewer than eight hundred permanent residents. For kayakers this port provides excellent access to Mansfield Pass and the islands and bayside communities of the Lower Laguna Madre.

Recommended Navigational Aids

Padre Island National Seashore, Texas #251, by Trails Illustrated; *Lower Laguna Madre* waterproof map by Hook-N-Line Map Company; aerial maps downloaded from TerraServer (www.terraserver.com), Google Earth (htp://earth.google.com), or MapQuest (www.mapquest.com).

Planning Considerations

Know when low tides are scheduled and avoid paddling the bay during these times. Also realize that high winds can affect water levels in this shallow bay system. Low tides, both predicted and those created by strong winds, can strand kayakers on shallow shorelines. The biggest hazard to paddlers is thunderstorms, which are common throughout the year, especially in the afternoons (see Hazards in the introduction to the book). Also, high winds and wind-generated waves in the deeper parts of Redfish Bay can pose a hazard on long open water crossings. Only the most experienced paddlers should attempt paddling on the open coast, depending on wind and wave action. If trying to make a beach landing on the outer coast, remember that during southeast winds there is often diminished wave action just north of the pass in the lee of the jetty. Be prepared to wait if conditions are unfavorable. Carry a cell phone and be prepared to contact one of the local guides to transport you back to Port Mansfield should you encounter sudden changes in conditions. In case of emergency, guides may be the best option for assistance or help may be obtained from the Willacy County sheriff in Port Mansfield at 956-689-5576. An honest and reliable guide familiar with transporting kayakers is Roger Kohutek of Rooster Charters (956-944-2150 or 956-642-7358, www.port-mansfield.com/rooster/Default.htm). A listing of guides is available online (www.port-mansfield.com/guide.htm). Although restaurants come and go, El Jefe's on the water just before the boat ramp is an excellent place to finish a trip. Experienced paddlers landing at the docks to eat have been known to roll their boats for beer!

Accommodations

In Port Mansfield the Adventures Lodge is on the water along the north side of the harbor and provides access to the water and facilities for cleaning fish and gear (956-944-4000, www.getawayadventureslodge.com). The Port Mansfield Sunset House is a short distance from the public boat ramp (956-944-2182, www.portmansfieldsunsethouse.com). Many condominiums are available close to Fred Stone County Park or on the harbor with access to the water. Contact the following for information: Cathy's Bay House Rentals (956-944-2575, www.cathysbayhouserentals.com), SeaWatch Realty (956-944-2800, www.seawatchrealty.net), and Y-Knot Bayhouse Rentals (956-944-2367, www.harborbait.com/lodging.htm).

Directions to Launch Sites

Port Mansfield: Take Highway 77 south from Kingsville (or north from Brownsville) to Highway 186 in Raymondville. Travel east on Highway 186 for approximately 24 miles to reach Port Mansfield. For trips to the south or to Mansfield Pass, turn right on South Port Road and stay right to merge onto Laguna Drive to access the public boat ramp and parking area on your left. For trips to the north, Highway 186 turns into Mansfield Road. Turn left along Bay Shore Drive (FM 606) to Fred Stone County Park. The park provides parking, a sandy beach for launching, and covered picnic shelters for day use only. In recent years the beach has become eroded, so watch for pieces of concrete and rock. A local spot that can be used for launching and landing can be reached by taking Matagorda Drive south from town. Turn left on a dirt road around the south side of a large earthen embankment. Follow the road around to the shoreline. This road is often muddy and there is a real risk of getting stuck. Follow the shoreline north to a shell beach or launch anywhere along the shore on the outer sand beach.

▲ *Kayakers landing in the dunes along Mansfield Pass.*

▶ *Beautiful gypsum crystals can often be found in the Mansfield area.*

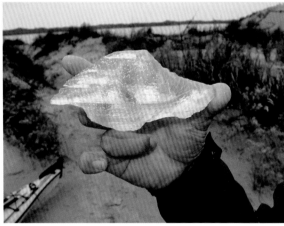

coming out of the east or southeast, wind-generated waves can make the area choppy and potentially unsuitable for beginners. Also, winds from the south or southeast can make the return trip much more difficult.

Cactus Island

INTERMEDIATE

3 miles

This spoil island is unnamed on maps but is a prominent feature about 1.5 miles east of Port Mansfield's harbor and just east of the intracoastal waterway. It is a great rest stop on longer trips and is a nice destination in itself. It can easily be reached from any of the launch sites at Port Mansfield. Notice the morphology of this island. The leading edge on the north side is eroded, with a cactus-covered bluff above, while the east and west flanks trail off to the south and form low-lying spits that surround a central shallow lagoon. The island has been shaped by the occasional but more severe storms coming out of the north rather than the more moderate prevailing winds out of the south and southeast. In recent years a breakwater has been built around the island to help prevent erosion. The higher parts of the island provide an excellent vantage point and are covered in prickly pear cactus, named the state plant in 1995. The pads or *nopales* are edible and are often grilled or included in soups and salads. I have never tried to eat the pads, but the bright red fruit is delicious when ripe, a great snack; be careful—it can stain your skin and clothes. Trailing off along the south side of the island are shallow oyster reefs that are fun to explore, but beware of the sharp oyster shells. Directly south beyond the Mansfield Pass channel is an often exposed oyster reef and bar frequented by pelicans and other shorebirds.

Bayshore North of Port Mansfield

BEGINNING

1–5 miles

Short trips north along the shoreline on calm days at high tides are good for birdwatching and fishing and are safe for beginners. Twin tanks less than 2.5 miles north of the county park are a good turnaround point and landmark (see later map of Padre Island National Seashore–Mansfield Pass route). If significant winds are

Padre Island National Seashore, Bayside Dune, and Mansfield Pass Trip

INTERMEDIATE TO ADVANCED

Day 1: 17.5–20.5 miles; Day 2–3: 9.5–12.5 miles

The duration of this trip is two to three days. It is not possible at low tides and requires good navigational skills. Be careful to check conditions before embarking as the trip begins with a 6.5-mile open water

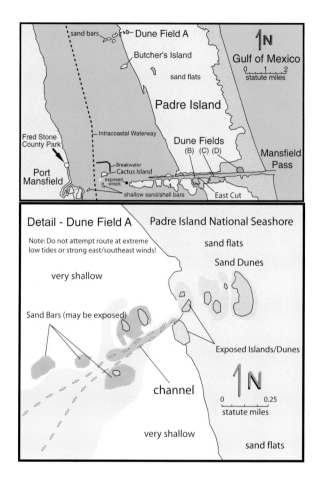

▲ *Small cactus-covered islands with relatively clear water are common in the Lower Laguna Madre, especially close to Mansfield Pass.*

◄ *An unnamed dune field north of Butcher's Island along the Lower Laguna Madre and the major dune fields along Mansfield Pass are signified by letters. The lower map shows details on the final approach.*

crossing. Park and launch at Fred Stone County Park. Set a compass heading of approximately 12–15 degrees north-northeast from the park. The bay side of Padre Island may not be visible. Keeping the correct heading, you should intersect the intracoastal waterway between piling markers #117 and #121. Check for ship traffic before crossing the waterway and remember that odd marker numbers line the east side of the channel. At this point you should be able to see the higher parts of Padre Island on the horizon and Butcher Island to your right.

On your approximate heading you should start to see the dune field in the distance rising above the horizon (see dune field *A* on map). Adjust your heading accordingly. As you get closer, use your paddle tips to check depth and stay in the channel approaching the island and dune formations (see detailed map). The sand flats form a broad expanse with little detail. When the water is calm, it may be difficult to see exactly where the water ends and the shore begins. Distances are deceiving. During times of very high water the dunes may form what appear to be islands. These dune fields are very different from the dune fields on the bay side along the Upper Laguna Madre. Few people see these dunes, as evidenced by the lack of trash or other signs of human activity. Deer, coyotes, rabbits, and other small mammals and a variety of birds may be seen here seasonally. Avoid walking on the dunes and vegetation. The bizarre dune formations and ghostly expanse of barren sand flats can make paddlers feel as if they are visiting another planet.

The next leg of the trip is approximately 8 miles. After resting on the shoreline, continue by paddling south-southwest toward the intracoastal waterway. Turn due south as the water becomes deep enough to paddle comfortably. Looking south as you pass Butcher Island, you will see Port Mansfield off in the distance to the right and on the left a series of islands that flank the south side of the East Cut to Mansfield Pass.

▶ *Bayshore dune fields north of Port Mansfield.*

▶▶ *Shorebirds feeding in the shallows near the dune fields north of Port Mansfield.*

Aim for the middle of the first island on the west side of this series of islands lining Mansfield Pass. As you get closer, you may see the remnants of an exposed wreck (an old barge) to the right of these islands. Stay to the left or east of the wreck (see detailed map). Rest on this island if necessary, or continue by turning east along the East Cut channel. On almost every trip through this channel to Mansfield Pass I have seen a pod of resident bottlenosed dolphins, which will approach kayakers if there is not too much boat traffic. This is the only place along the Texas coast where I have seen this behavior consistently. They often congregate around piling marker #13.

To continue, paddle due east along the East Cut channel 2.5 to 3.5 miles to reach dune fields *B* and *C* (see map). Currently it is acceptable to camp in these areas, as long as people practice leave-no-trace ethics and do not trample vegetation. I have often continued paddling through Mansfield Pass, where I have met family and friends who have driven 60 miles down the

seaward shoreline of Padre Island National Seashore. Primitive camping is also permitted north and south of the pass along the outer coast, which is often preferable during the hotter months. Beaches north and south inside the pass provide kayakers with a sheltered landing if necessary for camping on the seaward side of Padre Island.

It is well worth spending time exploring two dune fields along the south side of Mansfield Pass and a third field along the north side (see map, dune fields *B, C* and *D*). There are often fresh or brackish ponds that support more wildlife than in the dune field explored earlier well north of the pass. There are several small inlets to paddle into along the south side of the pass, especially when the water is high. In addition to birds and mammals, the red land crab (*Gecarcinus lateralis*) is a large and conspicuous resident of these communities. Vegetation is also more abundant and diverse.

Paddle back along the East Cut due west toward Port Mansfield. After passing the last island and the

◀ Juvenile dolphins are extremely playful and animated when active.

partially exposed wreck, head west-northwest toward Cactus Island before the intracoastal waterway. This island is approximately 1.5 miles off of Port Mansfield and makes a nice rest stop on the way back (see Cactus Island route). Continue west-northwest from the island back to Fred Stone County Park north of Port Mansfield.

Variations of this trip are as follows: A short day trip can be made to the cactus-covered island 1.5 miles off Port Mansfield. A day trip can be made to the northern dune field (13 miles, see dune field *A*). An overnight trip can also be made to Mansfield Pass (18 Miles, see next route).

▲ Dolphins airborne in Mansfield Pass early in the morning following a late November storm.

Mansfield Pass

INTERMEDIATE TO ADVANCED

Day 1: 6–9 miles; Day 2: 9–12 miles

This two-day trip is among the nicest along the coast. While there is a good deal of boat traffic on busy weekends, most of these people are consumed with fishing and seldom stop along the shore to explore. Watch for boat traffic out of the harbor and all along the East Cut to Mansfield Pass, especially when crossing the intracoastal waterway. Paddle east-northeast following the East Cut/Mansfield Pass piling markers across the intracoastal waterway. To the right of the channel after passing the intracoastal waterway is a small, often exposed oyster shell bar often covered in shorebirds and pelicans. Turn left to get to Cactus Island approximately 1.5 miles out. Land along the sandy beach along the west side of the island and climb up on the bluff to survey the surrounding area (see Cactus Island route).

Continue east along the channel past the exposed wreck of an old barge and then along the islands that flank the East Cut. At approximately 5 miles out along the islands, stop to explore the first small dune field (see map, dune field *B*). The vegetation is usually in bloom from June to October and can be spectacular.

Be careful not to trample the vegetation or dunes. If you walk south across the field, you can glimpse the extensive dune flats that line the back of Padre Island. Keeping an eye out for dolphins in the pass, continue paddling east less than a mile to the largest dune field in the pass (see map, dune field *C*). Stop here to explore this field. At present camping is permitted in both dune fields; be careful to practice leave-no-trace camping ethics here. Carefully climbing the tallest dune provides beautiful views from the outer coast of Padre Island and across the bay to Port Mansfield. Many paddlers decide to continue to the jetties at Mansfield Pass, where they camp on the seaward beaches of Padre Island either north or south of the jetties. This is a good choice during the hotter months. Beaches north and south just inside the pass provide kayakers with a sheltered landing if necessary for camping on the seaward beaches of Padre Island.

Paddling farther east along the cut brings you to

The crested caracara (Polyborus plancus) is often seen on the islands around Port Mansfield. Photo by Carmen Hagopian

a couple more inlets extending south of the channel that warrant exploration when water levels are high. These are excellent places for fishing and birdwatching. Turtles are often seen here in the shallows. Across on the north side of the channel is another dune field within the Padre Island National Seashore (see map, dune field *D*). Camping is not permitted here. This field is also accessible from the small four-wheel-drive road that extends from the north jetty. Paddling farther east out of the pass and into the Gulf of Mexico is complicated by unpredictable shoaling and, depending on the conditions, may be very dangerous. Before exiting the pass into open water, watch the wave sets for a while. The open water side of the north jetty is often sheltered and provides for easier beach landings when the wind is from the southeast. After camping on the outer coast or at one of the dune fields along the East Cut, paddle west again back to Port Mansfield.

Bennie's Shack

INTERMEDIATE

Day trip: 13–14 miles

This trip is one of the best along the Texas coast for birdwatching. The only exception is during duck hunting season, when airboats frequent the area. Paddle 0.75 mile east out of the Port Mansfield Harbor toward the intracoastal waterway. Avoid turning south after exiting the harbor as there are some shallow sand and shell bars that may not be passable. Turn south just before reaching the intracoastal waterway. Paddle south-southeast parallel to the piling markers just west of the intracoastal. After another 0.75 mile you will see a chain of spoil islands covered in vegetation. Keep an eye out for birds on these islands. After paddling another 4 to 4.5 miles you come to a cactus-covered island with a white cabin on stilts at the south end (see map, p. 108). This is Bennie's Shack and is private, but on the west side of the small island there is a bare central area where you can climb up and survey the surroundings. Directly west of the island is a wrecked barge on the shoreline. The property is private, but the beach is not, as it is technically part of the intertidal zone. Paddle west less than a mile to the barge on the beach. From here you can view large numbers of birds in the spring and fall in the wetlands behind the beach, but do not trespass without permission. If the water is high, you can paddle southwest along the shoreline and into the wetlands where the birds are. The detour can add 3–5 miles to the trip. After exploring, paddle back out of the shallows toward the intracoastal waterway and turn north again to return to Port Mansfield. ∎

Boca Chica State Park/Isla Blanca Park

OCA CHICA STATE PARK encompasses more than 1,000 acres between South Padre Island and the Rio Grande River, which forms the border with Mexico. This park was where the port of Brazos Santiago was once located, when the area was called Brazos Island. General Zachary Taylor had a supply depot there during the Mexican-American War in the late 1840s. The north end of the island was fairly well developed until most of it was destroyed in a severe storm in 1867.

Within the park, the shallow and often hypersaline South Bay provides a nursery ground for many marine invertebrates and fish as well as being an excellent place to observe coastal and migratory birds. Many interesting birds may be observed in this park, including Botteri's and Cassin's sparrows, reddish egrets, osprey,

roseate spoonbills, and aplomado and peregrine falcons. Sand dunes are interspersed with grassy vegetation, and prickly pear cactus and the Spanish dagger or Trecul's yucca plants are scattered throughout the park. The park also provides beach access to the Gulf of Mexico and Brazos Santiago Pass, where dolphins and sea turtles are commonly seen. The beach access for kayakers is far superior to the north side of the pass at Port Isabel. Fishing at the mouth of South Bay is known to be very good.

Brazos Santiago Pass and the adjacent ship channel connect Brownsville with commercial shipping and form the outlet for the southernmost terminus of the intracoastal waterway. Early attempts to keep Brazos Santiago Pass navigable were unsuccessful until granite jetties were constructed in 1935. Currently the pass and

The outer coast at Boca Chica State Park.

ship channel are maintained to a depth of 44 feet. The dredge spoil is predominantly high grade sand and is deposited 1 mile north of the jetty and 0.25–0.75 mile offshore to combat the serious erosion problems that South Padre Island faces. Cameron County's Isla Blanca Park on South Padre Island has a boat ramp that can be used to launch kayaks into Brazos Santiago Pass from South Padre Island. Although not as good an option as Boca Chica State Park, it is more convenient when staying at Port Isabel or on South Padre Island and does not require four-wheel-drive.

Recommended Navigation Aids

South Bay Paddling Trail Photomap by Shoreline Publishing; *Lower Laguna Madre* waterproof map by Hook-N-Line Map Company; aerial maps downloaded from TerraServer (www.terraserver.com), Google Earth (http://earth.google.com), or MapQuest (www.map quest.com)

Planning Considerations

Avoid low tides if you are planning to visit South Bay and beware of currents in the Brazos Santiago Pass during times of spring tides. Launching at the mouth of South Bay is not easy at low tide because of extensive mud flats. Only the most experienced paddlers should attempt paddling on the open coast, depending on wind and wave action. For security reasons, do not paddle up the Rio Grande and DO NOT camp in this park overnight.

Accommodations

Numerous accommodations are available at Port Isabel (www.portisabel.org), South Padre Island (www.spi chamber.com), and Brownsville (www.brownsville.org).

Directions to Launch Sites

Boca Chica State Park and Brazos Santiago Pass: From Brownsville, take Highway 4 approximately 22.5 miles to Boca Chica State Park. To bypass most of Brownsville if you are coming from the north, take FM 511 east from Highway 77. This road swings south and intersects with Highway 4. Turn left and proceed approximately 16.5 miles to get to the state park. No

entry fee is required. Drive into the park onto the beach facing the Gulf of Mexico. You can park anywhere along the beach to paddle along the open coast, but do not paddle south of the Rio Grande. To access Brazos Santiago Pass and South Bay, drive north to the jetties and turn west along a sandy road. You can either drive onto the beach adjacent to the pass and launch or continue west along the shoreline to the mouth of South Bay and launch. The beach adjacent to the pass is a much better place to launch as mud can be a problem along the mouth of South Bay, especially at low tide. Four-wheel-drive is usually necessary to access either place.

Alternatively, if you are staying at Port Isabel or on South Padre Island and do not wish to drive around to Boca Chica State Park, you can launch from the public boat ramp at Isla Blanca Park on South Padre Island.

Brazos Santiago Pass and Vicinity

INTERMEDIATE TO ADVANCED

variable mileage

Currents through the pass can be strong, especially during times of spring tides. In 1989 my wife and I

There are nice beaches facing South Padre Island at Boca Chica State Park, but a four-wheel-drive vehicle is recommended.

*The South Bay shoreline
at Boca Chica State Park.*

Side Trips

The University of Texas Pan American Coastal Studies Laboratory in Isla Blanca Park on South Padre Island has a small museum with aquarium displays worth visiting (866-441-UTPA, www.utpa.edu/csl). Also, in nearby Brownsville, Resaca de la Palma State Park is worth a visit for bird enthusiasts (956-585-9156, www.worldbirdingcenter.org/sites/brownsville). The Port Isabel Lighthouse (956-943-2262), Port Isabel Historic Museum (956-943-7602), and Treasures of the Gulf Museum (956-943-7602) are also worth seeing (all at portisabelmuseums .com).

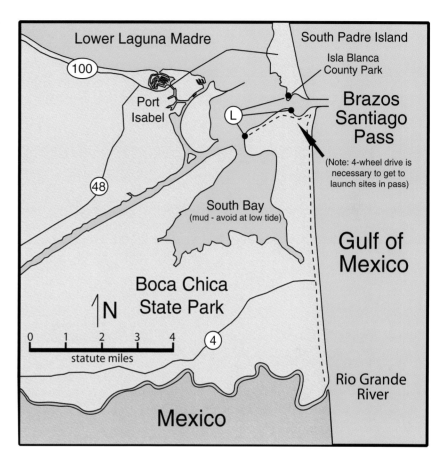

were kayaking across the channel in such a strong current that she was unable to paddle against it and was quickly being swept out into the Gulf of Mexico. I was fortunate to have a tow line, which allowed me to pull her into the eddy line along the south jetty. With great effort we averted disaster and landed on the beach behind the pass at Boca Chica State Park. At very low tides rocks are exposed on the north side of the pass near the lighthouse and are good for looking at intertidal animals and algae. These rocks are actually the ruins of an old lighthouse. You can almost always expect to see dolphins in the pass, and it is not uncommon to see sea turtles. More experienced paddlers can wander out to the terminus of the jetties and into the Gulf. In the summer and fall paddlers may see tarpon along and at the end of the jetties. I have seen their silvery backs exposed in the troughs of incoming waves, and they are often seen chasing schools of baitfish up close to the rocks. Paddling along the beach side of the Gulf of Mexico can be exciting but should be reserved for only the most experienced paddlers with good surf and rolling skills. However, on days when the surf is high and weather conditions are unfavorable, paddlers should stay out of the Gulf.

South Bay Paddle

BEGINNING TO INTERMEDIATE

up to 12 miles

The south bay loop follows the shoreline and GPS markers have been placed at intervals to aid in navigation. The markers are numbered 1–16 and were placed around the bay by Texas Parks and Wildlife. Approximate locations of the markers and GPS coordinates for each are given on a waterproof aerial photo map by Shoreline Publishing (see Recommended Navigation Aids). This estuary has extensive sea grass beds and oyster reefs; the reefs are primarily along the western side of the bay. There are many tidal creeks and parts of the shoreline are lined with mangroves. Fishing guides visit this area when water levels are high or during spring tides to fish for snook. The distance around the entire loop is approximately 11–12 miles. ■

Brazos Santiago Pass and South Bay in Boca Chica State Park. L designates launch sites. Be aware that a four-wheel-drive vehicle is required to access the launch sites within Boca Chica State Park. Below the beach, mud flats exposed during low tide make the launch site at the mouth of South Bay unusable.

Index

Other Titles in the Gulf Coast Books Series: